C·130

C·130
THE HERCULES

M. E. Morris

Presidio Press ★ **Novato, California**
THE PRESIDIO POWER SERIES
AIRPOWER #1009

Published by Presidio Press
31 Pamaron Way, Novato, CA 94949

Library of Congress Cataloging-in-Publication Data

Morris, M. E., 1926–
    C-130, the Hercules / M. E. Morris.
      p. cm. — (The Presidio power series. Airpower ; #1009)
    ISBN 0–89141–323–5
    1. Hercules (Turboprop transports)   I. Title.   II. Title: C-one
hundred thirty.   III. Series.
UG1242.T7M67—1988
358.4′4—dc19   88–17527
                                    CIP

Photo Credits:

Copyright © Marion E. Morris, pp. xi, xii, xiii, 24, 25, 26, 46, 57, 60, 61, 64, 70, 72, 79, 83, 85, 90, 94, 97, 105, 115, 121, 129
Copyright © John Gaffney, ii–iii, 27, 47, 49, 52, 63, 69
British Crown Copyright/Royal Aircraft Establishment Photograph, p. 104
Lockheed, pp. xiv, 7, 8, 9, 10–11, 13, 15, 19, 28, 34, 66, 68, 99, 100, 103, 107, 108, 112, 116, 118, 119, 122, 125
MarkAir Airlines, p. 111
Northwest Territorial Airlines, 113
U.S. Air Force, pp. i, vi–vii, 2, 4, 16, 18, 21, 22, 23, 31, 32, 33, 36, 37, 38, 40, 43, 44, 45, 48, 51, 55, 56, 58, 62, 88, 91, 92, 98, 124
U.S. Coast Guard, pp. 76, 80
U.S. Navy, pp. viii, x, 71

Printed in the United States of America

Contents

Acknowledgments

A number of very considerate and pleasant people have contributed to this work, among them Joe Dabney of Lockheed-Marietta, without whose assistance no definitive Hercules story can be told, and the folks at the news and media desks of the three military services and the USCG, who made it possible for me to update my flying experience with the modern day Herculeans.

But it is the men and women, military and civilian, who shared their experiences and expressed without reservation their admiration and faith in the Hercules as a flying machine who guided my hand as I tried to say what I so strongly feel.

To all of the above, too few of them recognized by name in this assemblage of words, I give my thanks and warmest wishes.

Preface

Probably no other aircraft has been examined by the printed word more than the Lockheed C-130 Hercules—and with good reason, for the airplane is indeed a classic. It has been in continuous production since 1954, if we use the roll-out date of the prototype for our measure. Lockheed-Marietta's Plant Number 6 still continues to complete an average of three Hercules every month and there is no sign of a slowdown. More than 1,800 C-130/L-100 aircraft have been produced, almost 1,000 for the U.S. Air Force alone. The Navy, Marine Corps, and Coast Guard also have significant numbers, and fifty-eight nations count the Hercules within their combined military and civilian inventory.

Indeed, with the development of their high technology test bed (HTTB—a C-130 look-alike), Lockheed seems determined to keep the aircraft in production forever. And as the Hercules finds ever new avenues of service to mankind, there will always be another story.

But there is a difference in the way the words are placed on these pages, for unlike the more clinical and detailed descriptive discussions preceding this account, almost all of them excellent in their portrayal of the many faces and deeds of this extraordinary aircraft, this is a love story.

I lived with my aluminum mistress for the better part of three years on the high, frozen deserts of Antarctica. We ate together, slept together, flew together, got scared out of our wits together, and matured into a relationship of mutual trust and respect (at least, I hope it was mutual) over some 1,200 hours of intimacy in the pure blue skies and on the deep white snows that cover the bottom of the earth.

I had first met her in Tennessee, where we were introduced by some mutual friends—the instructor staff of the 4442d Combat Crew Training Group at Sewart Air Force Base, blue-suiters who probably felt that a sky sailor was a bit out of his league in courting what was predominantly an air force amazon. Of course, I knew of her and had seen pictures of her, and had even danced with her once or twice, thanks to some squadron mates in the U.S. Navy's special mission squadron, VX-6 (later redesignated VXE-6). But we had never been formally introduced.

That came at Sewart. There, I first felt her come alive under my touch, and I under hers. We quickly formed a bond over those Tennessee hills, and started going steady. I learned all of her idiosyncrasies. I memorized her life systems. I studied the way she breathed, how she fed, and how she moved. I examined closely her circulation and her muscles. I listened to her heart; indeed, she has four and they provide her with a strength and rugged reliability that are matched only by her solid body.

We became lovers, in the sense that we were inseparable, and we moved through the next three years as one entity.

I shall never forget her, for in my forty years of flying she holds a singular place in my airman's soul. Together, we tasted the white blasts of antarctic blizzards; we rode the fierce turbulence of equatorial thunderstorms; we spanned oceans and continents; we held hands in the total darkness of many midnights and basked in a sun that never set. And on one occasion, completely out of our natural environment of snow and ice, we carried combat-hungry marines into the open jaws of a semitropical revolution.

My only regret is that she has had many lovers, and many of them have spent much more time with her than I, and gone through much worse ordeals. They will understand why I say these things and perhaps accept me as a member of their brotherhood.

There is an old Chinese proverb. Loosely translated it reads: A man is honored by his wife and children but it is only his mistress who never fails to place a smile upon his heart.

This is my tribute to the one who has always placed a smile upon my heart.

The *City of Christchurch* squats in the soft snow after its first landing to establish the site of America's most remote antarctic station. The pilot author surveys the plateau from the open crew entrance hatch.

Glossary

AAA Antiaircraft artillery.
ADS Air delivery system: all of the mechanical and electrical devices necessary to deliver airborne cargo.
AFB Air Force base.
AFRES Air Force Reserve.
AFROTC Air Force Reserve Officers Training Corps.
ANG Air National Guard.
ARRS Aerospace Rescue and Recovery Service/Squadron.
ART Air reserve technician: a member of a special civil service Air Force Reserve Program.
aspect ratio Ratio of wing span to wing median chord.
BDA Bomb damage assessor. A video device, which when coupled into the LLLTV system can be used to estimate bomb damage.
Black Crow Code name for sensor device to detect spurious radiation emissions.
BuNo Abbreviation of bureau number; the numerical ID assigned to each U.S. Navy/Marine Corps aircraft.
C-5 Four-jet-engined heavy airlifter (Lockheed).
C-7 Twin-engined assault transport (DeHavilland) used by U.S. Army and USAF.
C-82/119 Twin-engined, twin-boomed, cargo and troop carrier aircraft (Fairchild).
C-141 Four-jet-engined airlifter (Lockheed).

CAVU Ceiling and visibility unlimited.
CDS Container delivery system: a C-130 airdrop system for special palletized cargo.
CH-54 Sikorsky-built cargo helicopter.
Combat Talon Designation of modified C-130 used in USAF Special Operations.
CUT The signal given a carrier pilot that tells him he is in position for, and cleared for, landing.
CVA U.S. Navy attack carrier.

A Clearwater, Florida, USCG Hercules drives through the plane wash after a nine-hour drug interdiction patrol over the Gulf of Mexico, the fresh water washing away the corrosive salt spray.

Hercules Pave Spectre gunship at Eglin AFB, Florida.

DEEPFREEZE Annual U.S scientific operation in Antarctica.

DEW Detection and early warning radar system.

ECM Electronic countermeasures.

eshp Estimated shaft horsepower.

FAA Federal Aeronautics Administration. Also Fuerza Aerea Argentina (Argentine Air Force) in this text.

FAR Federal aviation regulations.

FLIR Forward-looking infrared sensor system.

g Gravitational force (normally 1 g).

GCA Ground Controlled Approach using radar and radio guidance.

GPES Ground proximity extraction system: a hook and catch-cable system of extracting cargo from a low flying aircraft.

HF High frequency radio waves.

HH-3E Rescue and recovery helicopter (Sikorsky).

HOW Hercules-on-Water development program testing the feasibility of an amphibian C-130.

HTTB High technology test bed: Lockheed's research C-130, used to develop and test advanced concepts of Hercules control and utilization.

HU-25A USCG patrol version of Falcon executive jet transport (Dassault-Breguet).

IAS Indicated air speed.

Ice Colloquialism for Antarctica.

IFR Instrument flight rules.

INS Inertial navigation system.

LAPES Low altitude parachute extraction system: a component of the PLAD system of air cargo delivery.

LLLTV Low light level television: a TV camera system capable of obtaining identifiable imagery within an extremely low-level-of-light environment.

Loran Longe range aerial navigation system.

MAC Military Airlift Command.

MATS Military Air Transport Service.

NATS Naval Air Transport System.

NROTC Naval Reserve Officers Training Corps.

NVG Night vision goggles featuring battery-powered light amplification circuitry.

ODS Overhead delivery system: a system of extracting cargo from an airborne C-130 using overhead guide rails.

Pave Low Designator of helicopter used in rescue and recovery operations.

Pave Pronto Special C-130 gunship employing Black Crow sensor.

AFRES Hercules makes an assault landing on dirt strip at the U.S. Army's Pinon Canyon Exercise Range, Colorado.

Pave Spectre   One of several C-130 gunship configurations.

PLAD   Parachute low-altitude delivery system: devices and tactics used to airdrop cargo at low altitudes.

Psyops   Psychological warfare operations.

SAM   Surface-to-air missile.

SAR   Search and rescue.

Spectre   Code name for C-130 gunship.

STAR   Fulton-designed personnel recovery system used by airborne C-130 aircraft to retrieve downed personnel.

Starlifter   USAF Lockheed C-141 airlift aircraft.

STOL   Short-field takeoff and landing.

TACAMO   Acronym for take-charge-and-move-out: a code name assigned to U.S. Navy special communications air squadrons.

UHF   Ultra-high frequencies.

URGENT FURY   U.S. military operation involved in 1983 Grenada invasion.

USAFR   United States Air Force Reserve.

VHF   Very high frequencies.

VX-6/VXE-6   U.S. Navy's special mission air logistic squadron tasked with support of scientific research in Antarctica.

WINFLY   Late winter logistic flight(s) flown from Christchurch, New Zealand, to McMurdo Station, Antarctica.

WRS   Weather reconnaissance service or squadron.

Chapter 1
In the Beginning . . .

Hercules.
  When the supreme god of Greek mythology, the mighty Zeus, seduced the lady Alcmene, wayward wife of Amphitryon, he must have been quite pleased with himself. His bastard son was the very personification of strength and power, a god-man who would forever be the symbol of the strongest of the strong. But Zeus would probably have thrown in a couple more thunderbolts during his lovemaking with Alcmene if he had known that centuries later a small team of mere mortals would give birth to another Hercules whose feats would surpass even those of his son.

That more mortal Hercules, conceived with equal passion by the members of the Advanced Design Department of Lockheed Aircraft Corporation at Burbank, California, would influence the lives of earthlings in a much more widespread and practical way than its mythical namesake. The earthly Hercules would touch every corner of the world in a very real manner.

An aerial classic fulfilling the most stringent definition of the word, the Lockheed C-130 aircraft is a contradiction within the streamlined, needle-nosed, thin-winged world of contemporary aviation. A one-of-a-kind combination of thick, aerodynamic curves and raw power, the sausage-shaped Hercules waddles like an overweight caterpillar whenever it moves along the surface of the earth. But let it raise its fat snout and enter its natural habitat — the skies over our blue planet — and the caterpillar becomes a butterfly soaring heavenward on outstretched wings that support a belly full of whatever you want. With the smooth power of its four turboprop engines filling the air with the unmistakable throaty hum of its mighty voice, the Hercules doesn't claw its way into the sky as did its predecessors. It *soars* — and climbs on its way in great sweeping rises and long cruising flights that make it seem as much a natural body in the sky as the sun and the moon and the clouds and the stars. It is a great multicolored bird with a skin of smooth aluminum stretched across its incredibly strong metal skeleton. It moves across continents and oceans, over both poles, around the equator, through the clouds, under the stars. There is only one rule of its existence: Wherever there is sky, there is Hercules. Zeus himself must

Reaching up into its natural habitat for the first time, the prototype YC-130 leaves Burbank Airport on August 23, 1954.

sit in his mythical heaven and marvel.

And well he might, for the Lockheed C-130 Hercules is one of that rare breed of flying machines that has exceeded its design specifications and proved to be much more than a studied collection of parts devised and assembled according to a series of aerodynamic laws. Every so often, a mysterious and unknown quality slips into the calculations of aeronautical engineers and the skillful hands of accomplished airmen that gives their airborne steed a special capability that enables it to fulfill much more than its original mission. The aircraft operates beyond its design bounds and has an influence on mankind itself. Such is the Hercules, for it is much more than a machine of war. It is a humanitarian, an economist, an explorer, and an internationally known symbol of America's technical creativeness and sympathetic heart. Its feats are legendary and it would take volumes just to recount them.

Somewhere within the Hercules there seems to be an astounding intangible, an ability as it were to exceed itself. Perhaps we can think of it as soul. How did it get there? The practical mind concludes that it is just a fortunate happenstance of design and engineering. But should we not wonder? Could Zeus himself have had a hand in the creation of his son's namesake?

We reached the end of World War II with no real tactical airlift aircraft, at least not in the sense of an airplane that had been specifically designed to carry and deliver machines and men of war. True, we had extracted yeoman service from a bevy of converted civilian transports — C-47s, C-46s, C-54s, C-121s, and dozens of lesser designs. And we did have the Fairchild C-82 Packet, a 1944 attempt to come up with

an airlift aircraft (more about that later). But we carried cargo in airplanes that had been built to haul people and had little bulk loading space, although they could lift respectable weights in their time. For loading and off-loading, however, their makeshift cargo compartments were either on a tilt due to a tail-gear configuration, or the cargo-loading opening was too high for efficient access. As for vehicular transportation, even something as small and light as a Jeep presented a logistical problem if it was to be shipped by air. Something as massive and heavy as a main battle tank was out of the question. As for dropping troops, the World War II workhorses were capable, but the placement of their wide horizontal tail planes was less than attractive to the men hurling themselves out the jump door.

World War II troops file aboard a Curtiss C-46 Commando. Designed primarily as a personnel carrier, the tough C-46 was awkward to load with heavy or big bulk cargo.

All other phases of aerial warfare had measurably progressed. We started World War II with the P-40, the F4F Wildcat, and the B-17 bomber. By the time those top-hatted Japanese made their long climb up the USS *Missouri*'s boarding ladder in Tokyo Bay, we had the P-51, the F6F and F4U Corsair, and the B-29. We could fire rockets as well as bullets and drop a nuclear explosive device in place of iron bombs. But we were still dropping cargo and troops from prewar C-47s.

Our airlift specialists in the newly created U.S. Air Force of 1947 were acutely aware of the situation. And as if they needed a reminder, the Soviets challenged them with the closing of surface routes into Berlin (see Chapter 2 for a few more words on this subject). Close on the heels of that crisis came the Korean conflict, in which we were not only faced with a requirement for logistic airlift, we had an urgent need for tactical airlift. Our cold war was very hot.

Once again, we didn't have a single aircraft designed for military airlift that could accomplish its tactical mission with combat efficiency and an acceptable degree of safety. And to add despair to our misery, we really needed something that could operate off of unprepared surfaces. True, the C-82 and its somewhat larger brother, the C-119 Flying Boxcar, were attempts as such machines, but their forward area capability was limited and the loss of an engine when carrying a combat load turned them into flying bricks.

The outbreak of that celebrated "police action" in Korea placed immediate emphasis on our urgent need for battlefield tactical airlift. Thus, in January 1951, the USAF's Tactical Airlift Command (TAC) began to define their concept of a medium-class cargo- and troop-carrying transport. They followed their studies with requests for proposals to the big three American aircraft manufacturing companies, Boeing, Douglas, and Lockheed, and also Fairchild, who had designed and produced the C-119.

Overall, the USAF wanted an airplane that would have the capability of carrying 30,000 pounds of cargo over intratheater distances or deliver ninety assault troops or airdrop seventy-two paratroopers on nonstop flights that would range 2,000 miles. The aircraft must be capable of hauling bulky as well as heavy equipment, with a cargo compartment measuring at least forty feet long, ten feet wide, and nine feet high. Since troops would be carried in that same space, it must be pressurized, for the USAF wanted an aircraft that could fly high above the weather and ground fire. A cabin altitude of not more than 8,000 feet must be maintained.

For ease of loading and unloading, the cargo deck had to be at the same level as the standard U.S. truck bed and the access had to provide for a roll-on, roll-off capability. Not only that, the ramp that gave the aircraft its loading convenience had to be operable in flight for airdropping large cargo units.

Dependable controllability had to be a feature, for the aircraft would be dropping paratroopers at slow speeds (125 knots) and they would require a stable platform for their rapid, low-level egress. For ground delivery, the aircraft would have to be able to operate from bare-base locations; clay, sand, and humus were listed as probable landing surfaces.

Finally, the loss of an engine could not jeopardize the mission. It was intended that the aircraft would be operated within a hostile ground environment.

The Fairchild-Hiller C-119 Flying Boxcar set the pattern for a roomy cargo compartment with rear loading doors and a close-to-ground profile. A versatile performer, later versions saw duty as AC-119 G/K gunships.

For their part, the Lockheed design engineers, under the superb leadership of Willis Hawkins, wanted to stress primarily simplicity of form, reliability of operation, and rugged strength to withstand the rigors of combat flying and unprepared field delivery. A secondary aim was to come up with a design that could be manufactured, operated, and maintained economically in terms of parts and manpower expenditure.

The more the engineers examined the specifications required by the USAF, the more they realized that the design of the airplane was in part already established by the air force specs. The requirement for such a large cargo compartment, with rapid and convenient on-loading and off-loading, dictated a long box, similar in dimensions to a boxcar. They would have to wrap it within a cylinder for strength and streamlining and provide for a pass-through main wing spar.

But the plane's basic shape was predetermined. To keep the cargo compartment clear, they decided on a high wing, above the space. And that wing would have to provide very efficient, high-speed lift and low-speed approach and landing stability. Long range called for a high-aspect-ratio wing, such as that used on the B-24 of World War II fame, and an aspect ratio of 10:1 was decided upon. With a 132-foot span and a tapered plan profile that created a wing area of 1,745.5 square feet, the plane would have an acceptable wing loading of 61.9 pounds of lift per square foot at a total aircraft weight of 108,000 pounds.

The wide fuselage, shaped around the rectangular cargo compartment, would provide for a roomy flight deck forward. A design bonus was a cockpit compartment that offered the best visibility of any transport aircraft and allowed space for the crew members to walk around and stretch on long flights. A flight-deck crew of four was envisioned: pilot, copilot, flight engineer, and navigator. A fifth crew member, the aircraft's loadmaster, would man the cargo space.

The main landing gear had to withstand assault landings, and the retracting and housing mechanism could not intrude into the cargo compartment. The landing gear couldn't be dropped from the high wing; it would be too unstable, too heavy, and subject to unacceptable stress. In an innovative approach typical of the design team's intention to let their imagination and creative impulses roam unhampered by conventional thinking, the Lockheeders decided to place the main gear *outside* the cargo section of the fuselage. This would also allow them to utilize vertical landing gear struts, simple in design and ingenious in concept, since the landing loads could be carried first by the massive struts, then if need be by the fuselage strength members, and in extremis on up to the powerful wing structure. The drag would be kept down by placing the four wheels in tandem, two to a side, with high-flotation, low-pressure tires for effective ground handling. The tandem arrangement would also allow the forward wheels to break ground and pack a path for the rear wheels on unprepared surfaces. A dual-nose wheel installation, with the wheels side by side but with similar tires, completed the arrangement.

The selection of the number and type of engines was a major consideration. In a decision that would become typical of Lockheed's forward-thinking Advanced Design Department (which later would produce such superb performers as the F-104, the U-2, and the still-extraordinary SR-71), the engineers selected the Allison turboprop T56A-1 engine, rated at 3,750 eshp (estimated shaft horsepower). Four of them would be needed so that a loss of one would not compromise the aircraft's mission. The newly created turboprop design would provide economical and fast cruise at altitude, and all-around dependability over the more complex and multi-parted conventional internal combustion aircraft engines still in widespread use in the early fifties.

The engineers decided to mate the Allisons with Curtis-Wright three-bladed, full-reversible, full-feathering propellers. The union of the constant-speed turboprop engines and the quick-pitch-change capability of the propellers would provide the rapid acceleration and deceleration capability that would be lacking with the pure turbojet engine, which was just coming into its own on almost all other military aircraft.

The result was Lockheed's Temporary Design

Designation L-206. In keeping with their tradition of naming their aircraft for stars and constellations as well as their consideration of the rugged strength of the mythical Greek hero, the company gave its new aircraft a most apt name: Hercules.

The Air Force liked the Lockheed concept and in September 1952 awarded contracts for two prototype YC-130 aircraft. The Lockheed design and engineering team, with Art Flock as project engineer, began its task in earnest. While the two prototypes would be manufactured in Lockheed's Burbank plant, the production facility would be in their huge assembly complex at Marietta, Georgia. While the main thrust of Lockheed's effort was in the expeditious production of the prototypes, advance parties from Marietta proceeded to Burbank to study the development of the prototypes and prepare themselves to guide the efforts at Marietta for the construction of the six development aircraft, a single test specimen, and the twenty production C-130s called for in the initial USAF contracts.

The roll-out of the prototype YC-130 in August 1954 created an inordinate amount of dinner conversation within the aviation world. While the first photographs of the concept had been released as far back as February 1953, the first three-dimensional public view of the Hercules caused some people to conclude that Lockheed had slipped its corporate gears. Accustomed to sleek company designs such as the wartime P-38 Lightning and the postwar P-80 Shooting Star, certain segments of the aviation crowd raised skeptical eyebrows at the fat, silver bird that was towed out onto the hardtop. Many understood at that moment why Lockheed's own Kelly Johnson, one of their star engineers, had refused to even sign Lockheed's original proposal to the Air Force.

The critics couldn't help but marvel, however, at the completeness of the design. Right away, the lower cockpit windows caught their attention. The pilots could see *down* as well as forward and around. The better to spot drop sites and taxi over rough terrain, explained Lockheed. There was even a fifth engine! — an internal auxiliary power plant tucked away in the forward bulge of the port main landing gear blister. The aircraft carried its own ground support power.

The tall, upswept tail with the tip of the fin some thirty-eight feet above the hardtop was an immediate attention getter. The afterfuselage had an elongated cylindrical cross section that incorporated a two-piece loading ramp and cargo door. When closed, the pair meshed perfectly with the underside of the fuselage. When open, the forward portion dropped down to become a horizontal loading platform while the rearmost door retracted upward completely out of sight. More than that, the cargo loading ramp could even be lowered from its horizontal position to rest on the surface of the landing area for instant roll-off of vehicles. The result was unobstructed full-dimensional access to the cavernous cargo compartment by troops, cargo pallets, heavy equipment, and vehicles.

Also noteworthy were two separate paratrooper exit doors, one on each side of the after cargo bay, with retractable wind-deflector plates, which would make the troopers' airborne egress more safe and less traumatic. Ahead of each

Fighter jocks of the fifties took a close second glance at the big bird invading their high-altitude domain. The prototype YC-130 introduced a new shape to the stratosphere and the giggles soon turned into wide smiles of admiration.

7

door were racks for four solid-rocket thrust boosters to expedite short-field or heavy-load takeoffs. A crew entrance hatch was lowered on the port side forward, its inner lining providing crew boarding steps. Perhaps, thought a few of the at-first-dubious onlookers, there was a bit more to the Hercules than met the eye!

Still, much of the secret of the aircraft's potential was inside the machine and not noticed at first glance. A great portion of the strength and reliability of the Hercules was contained in its guts. First of all there was the massive wing box incorporating machined panels forty-eight feet long. By using the new A78S-T aluminum alloy extensively throughout the basic construction, primarily for large cast and machined parts, Lockheed had gained seven percent more stress absorption while affecting a significant reduction in weight over previous alloys. In many areas,

The blunt-nosed Hercules soon became the pilots' favorite and the waiting lines at Marietta began to grow as the C-130As entered the Air Force inventory.

Eat your hearts out, Thunderbirds! USAF Captains Gene Chaney, William Hatfield, James Akin, and David Moore (*l.-r.*) flew as The Four Horsemen flight demonstration team of the 463d Troop Carrier Wing.

metal bonding was used, another relatively new weight-saving process.

A superb web of control and system redundancy was built into the C-130. The flight controls were hydraulically boosted by two separate and independent systems, each system pressurized by two independent hydraulic pumps. System pressure was an astounding (for that era) 3,000 psi. Included within the primary boost system, for example, were hydraulic pumps driven by engines one and three — the outboard left and inboard right. The utility system was serviced by pumps on engines two and four — inboard left and outboard right. Any single engine pump could provide hydraulic pressure for all three flight controls (elevator, rudder, and aileron). The utility system provided pressure for operation of the landing gear, flaps, brakes, and nose-gear steering.

Lockheed backed up their hydraulically boosted control system by installing electrically operated trim tabs on all three axes (pitch, yaw, and roll) and powering them with DC generators (five — one on each engine and another on the air turbine motor). The tabs could also be powered by the aircraft's batteries. Should everything fail (!) the C-130 could be manually flown at low speeds. Recognizing that leg strength is superior to arm strength, the thoughtful engineers installed foot braces at the bottom of the pilot's and copilot's instrument panels to provide them a means of added leverage for man-hauling the control yokes fore and aft. All of the Hercules control systems simply do not fail, however, and the handy appendages were destined to become convenient footrests for crew comfort on long flights. There breathes not a C-130 pilot who has not availed himself — or herself in more recent years — of that relaxed legs-up posture. But

who is to say that in some distant year a completely powerless C-130 will not descend to a safe landing controlled by a sweating aviator with his feet braced against those sturdy supports? Certainly, that remote capability is built into the airplane.

The U.S. Air Force specifications also called for internal heating, cooling, and ventilation with the main engines shut down. The auxiliary power unit, more properly referred to as the auxiliary gas turbine (AGT), mounted in the forward port main gear housing, provided this capability, and in addition supplied high-pressure air for main engine starts. The AGT also drove the air turbine motor (ATM), which in turn drove a DC generator and an emergency hydraulic pump. As a further example of ingenious design, the ATM and the emergency hydraulic pump could also be

Up, up, and away! The first C-130A production airplane lifts its blunt proboscis and introduces a new era of tactical airlift. The date: April 7, 1955.

11

driven by bleed air directed from any one of the four main engines.

Crew comfort considerations included a small galley facility on the after port side of the flight deck, two urinals aft behind the paratrooper exit doors, and a chemical toilet hung from the side of the fuselage back by the cargo loading ramp.

Thus, the prototype Hercules, squatting there on the sunlit ramp at Burbank, was a quantum jump over any previous logistic and tactical airlift vehicle, despite its Durante nose and rather obese shape.

In many respects, the morning of August 23, 1954, was like any southern California morning. The coastal fog, mixed with the ever-present man-made air pollutants, blanketed the entire Los Angeles area, including the Burbank airport. Stanley Beltz, Lockheed's chief test pilot for the Hercules project, tried hard to hide his impatience, as did his crew of Roy Wimmer, copilot, and flight engineers Jack Real and Dick Stanton. On the ramp sat YC-130 Number 53–3397, ready to go. But this was a normal morning and Beltz knew that as soon as the sun rose higher and a bit of a sea breeze stirred, the fog would dissipate. And five hours later, it did.

Now, design specs are one thing, and a pretty airplane can show lots of promise just by its poise and eye appeal. But every pilot knows that the real test comes when he straps the machine to his rear and takes it into the air. Only then will he and others know just how well their creation flies. The proof of the pudding is in the tasting, and on this California morning, Beltz was quite ready to taste the flavor of the Lockheed concoction that looked unlike anything he had ever flown. Of course, he knew the Hercules like his own body and could trace its systems as well as he could tell you about his own bloodstream. He had lived with the Hercules since it had been conceived and had been in effect its male midwife at its birth. Now it was time to slap its rear and see how it responded. And Stanley Beltz was a pilot's pilot and typical of the Lockheed clan that had a reputation for putting an aircraft through its paces, no holds barred. With a look and build that could have made him a contender as a middleweight boxer, he squinted his pug nose and studied the clearing sky.

The senior pilot always gets the publicity, and perhaps rightly so since he is the one responsible for instant decisions that can spell the difference between glory and disintegration, but Beltz knew that he was backed up by fellow professionals in the copilot and flight engineer seats. With a plane as complicated as this multiengined flying machine, one man can fly it, but it takes several to operate it.

The crew, in turn, knew that some of the best minds in aviation had drawn the lines and engineered the systems that made up the tantalizing airplane sitting before them. Wind-tunnel tests had modified the engineers' drawings, and final calculations had produced a set of performance figures that were hard to believe. But something was in the air. Beltz had a feeling that he and his crew were about to taste a gourmet meal.

Under his guiding hands and those of his crew,

The Hercules has gained a worldwide reputation for hauling anything anywhere, anytime. Irreverently dubbed ''Trash-hauler'' by its proud crews, the Herk flies on all seven continents.

the four turboprop engines whined to life. Every Lockheed employee who could tear himself away from his job watched the Hercules start to breathe and then move. There *was* a certain magnificence in its slow gait. And there was an almost insufferable delay as the crew put the airplane through its preflight engine and systems checks. Then it was on the runway.

Beltz advanced the power levers, and the fire roaring in the four combustion chambers intensified. Instantly, tiny power-sensing devices sent signals to the electric motors governing the propeller blades and they set themselves at precise angles to balance the power of the engines with their bite into the air. So precisely was the system designed that the engine turbines remained at a constant speed, and would remain so throughout the flight of the Hercules. That was one of the secrets of the anticipated rapid acceleration — a responsive prop blade change to the changing power of the constant-speed engines. And did it ever work!

The crew felt the acceleration instantly as the Hercules surged forward, pressing them against the backs of their seats. Beltz shifted his guiding hand from the nosewheel steering wheel to the yoke and gave a few tentative pulls and turns, then allowed the nosewheels to clear the runway. Hercules wanted to fly! But behind Beltz's high forehead, crowned with an ample cap of curly hair, there was the common sense mixture of daring and caution that was a hallmark of Lockheed test pilots. He felt out the controls, then pulled back his power levers into the reverse pitch range and reined his charging mount to a halt. His grin was even wider as he swung the Hercules around and tried another trial run back up the runway, taking the Hercules just to the point where *it was ready!* There was no doubt

that the pioneer crew had a tiger by the tail, but one whose aggressive charge was tempered with a gentle feel for the business that it would soon be about. Once more, Beltz lowered the nose and air-braked to a stop. It was time.

Another precise lineup, a positive application of the power levers to full thrust, a subdued chuckle as the seat back pressed him forward, and a shift of his left hand from the nosewheel steering wheel to the yoke. A gentle pull and the blunt nose rose. The Hercules lifted and entered its more natural realm. They were only 855 feet down the runway and barely eight seconds had elapsed since Beltz had released the brakes.

After a cautious cleanup, he established his climb and felt the thrill of unanticipated power and grace as the C-130 rose over Burbank. Beltz later would state that he had trouble keeping his airspeed down as the Hercules reached for the heavens. That was not news to the flight crew of the chase plane, a P2V Neptune. A typically sleek, sister Lockheed design, and certainly no climb slouch for its day, the Neptune was hard-pressed to match the Hercules' climb rate! Far below, those being rapidly left behind on the ground felt the chill of success as they recognized that they were witnessing something special.

There is an unimaginable thrill of a first flight in a completely new aircraft. No matter how professional the crew, or how serious they take their specific test duties, there is a unique little-boy emotion of the realization of "Hey! I'm the first one to be up here in this thing!" When "this thing" is as large and innovative as the first Hercules, the thrill must approach the limits of tolerability.

But Beltz and his crew had much to do. Level-

ing off at 10,000 feet, they ran through a series of basic checks. They cycled the landing gear, feeling out the trim and drag changes. They did the same with the flaps, trying various settings and noting — with extreme pleasure — the inherent stability in the airplane. Then the approaches to a stall, and the stall itself. That was an all-important task, for Beltz and his crew would not be returning to Burbank. So confident was the Lockheed team of the reliability of their baby, they had programmed it to be delivered to Edwards Air Force Base on its initial flight.

The low-speed handling characteristics were excellent, and with every confidence Beltz headed inland for Edwards. Sixty-one minutes later, he set the Hercules down with an impressive

The First Lady, who led all other production Hercules off the Marietta production line. In 1989 she flies into her 34th year.

short-field approach that would later cause him to claim he could have landed it *across the runway.* Disembarking in front of the air force brass, Beltz could hardly stop talking about the airplane. Always a supremely confident test pilot, he almost popped right out of his flight suit with enthusiasm.

The anticipatory air force airmen looked at the C-130 as if they were being introduced to a blind date who apparently had a great personality but should lay off the between-meal snacks.

Hercules had arrived.

15

Chapter 2
Logistic Airlift

Maybe we should thank the Soviets instead of Zeus for triggering the creation of Hercules. When the former closed down all avenues of access to Berlin on June 28, 1948, except for three precarious air corridors, the Allies were faced with the biggest lift requirement that had ever challenged aviation. It is to our everlasting credit, and that of our staunch allies, the British (who even hired private air contractors and included in their service forces their workhorse Sunderland flying boats and converted bombers), that we met the challenge with an epic airlift that has a unique place in military history. Mustering every tired C-47, overworked C-54 (and R5D), and hump veteran C-46 we could lay our hands on, as well as a handful of C-82 Packets, we and our friends put three solid streams of aircraft into beleaguered Berlin and kept them flowing for more than eleven months. The airmen of MATS and NATS, along with the equally determined Brits, performed a herculean task (no pun intended; remember, the C-130 was still six

years away). And lest it be overlooked, we should remember that the aerial bridges into Berlin involved the manpower of not only the U.S. and the United Kingdom (with flight crews from Australia, New Zealand, and South Africa as well as the RAF), but 45,000 German cargo loaders and airfield workers, 3,000 Baltic displaced persons, and a number of French civilians from their military agencies. And perhaps there was a glimpse of the potential of airlift when a single Douglas C-124 Globemaster (later to be affectionately dubbed the Aluminum Overcast) made twenty-four flights to Berlin during the period from August 17 to 24 September, carrying up to twenty tons per trip. But what a shame Hercules was not there to help. Their flights could have been cut by almost two-thirds and the off-loading crews could have sold most of their high-reaching forklifts and A-frames for well-deserved beer money. Where it took seven C-47s, each struggling to keep up to 6,000 pounds of cargo airborne and leaking gallons of oil across eastern Germany, a single Hercules would have sufficed. A lone C-130E could have easily replaced two C-54s or four C-82s — or easily equalled the per-trip tonnage of the much larger Globemaster! The three streams of aircraft into Berlin could have been thinned and speeded up at the same

Insignia of the United States Air Force Military Airlift Command, the world's largest and most far-reaching air transport service.

Fighter, explorer, and humanitarian, the versatile Hercules is instantly recognized by millions of people who have benefited from its use.

pace that on occasion necessitated aircraft arriving within seconds of each other.

Having said that, a caveat should be added. After all, one can "prove" almost anything with figures, and the above statements were based primarily on the load-carrying capacity of the C-130E versus that of the other involved aircraft. Do a bit of division and you come up with 121 C-130s. But we all know that there were other considerations, and it may be that 125 C-130s or even 150 would have been needed. Whatever the figure, the point is that our logistic airlift capability today is head and shoulders above what it was in those trying days of 1948.

Ask any veteran of Vietnam who watched the lumbering Hercules scream down from its en route altitude above the ground fire and slam onto a shell-pocked rough strip in what appeared to be more of a controlled crash than anything else, and he'll tell you what a welcome sight it was to see the "trash haulers" arrive. For him, it was literally a matter of life and death. But don't *you* and *I* refer to the Herk by that name — not unless we were there — for trash hauler is a treasured term of endearment and typical of irreverent monikers the military seems to like to hang on things it loves the most. Sort of like saying "the ole woman" when talking about a better half.

And every Herk ever made, whether it be an A model or a B, an E, or an H, starts out with a heritage as a trash hauler; it'll carry anything anywhere, any time.

time and the aircrews could have been spared countless cases of high blood pressure and debilitating fatigue. Not that it wouldn't have been an effort. No, indeed, for more than 2,323,067 tons of life-sustaining supplies were delivered to the Berliners between that fateful day in June 1948 and the last official resupply flight on May 12, 1949. Even for the Hercules, that would have been a respectable task.

Nevertheless, instead of the 586 U.S. and British aircraft employed in the airlift, the operation could have been conducted with 121 C-130Es at a "leisurely" pace of one delivery per airport every thirty-six minutes (Templehof in the U.S. sector, Gatow in the British sector, and Tegel in the French sector were all utilized). Instead, the task required an eleven-month backbreaking

Leo J. Sullivan leans back in his chair, overpowering it with rugged bulk, shirtsleeves rolled a couple of turns up over his forearms. Within the Lockheed-Georgia organization he carries the title of Assistant to Chief Engineer-Design — one of those titles that the bureaucracy gives to the world's best pilots when they transition them from the cockpit to the office. It's the inevitable promotion that all good pilots fear. And Sullivan's desk reflects his good-natured resolution to the situation. It features what can most charitably be called organized clutter, with several pieces of interrupted business lying just before him, ignored while he speaks of his true love, flying. Pictures are on all the walls around him, telltale depictions of his past and present. A large hard-plastic model of a P2V Neptune sits on a small cabinet behind him, one prop with a blade missing. Leo has a cherished naval aviator heritage and he warms to the task of giving an interview when he learns I share a background in navy patrol boats.

Leo Sullivan is one of the vanishing breed of American airmen who cut their teeth on a hundred or so different aircraft. His list covers a single page with several columns and he grants me a singular honor by letting me review it. I feel he doesn't do that with everyone. They'd mistake his pride for ego. Not me. I know that the long tabulation of aircraft, from tiny drones to the massive C-5, represents a very valuable human lifetime within the eighty-five-year span of what we know as aviation. There will be no more Leo Sullivans. The technology is too advanced now. If a man learns to fly a dozen different aircraft well, he is in the forefront of his profession. The young bucks who drive the F-16s and F-18s around the thin air above our planet, many of them future test pilots, are sophisticated technicians whose grasp of the intricacies of modern flight control and weapons systems requires formal education and training far beyond

what was demanded of Sullivan and his contemporaries. Leo, of course, is an outstanding engineer and technician, but basically he is a stick-and-rudder man and the Hercules cut its first teeth under his guiding grasp. They learned about each other together.

The day was April 14, 1955, and the place was Dobbins Air Force Base in Marietta, Georgia. The first production aircraft to fly, Number 53–3129, lifted into the still spring air with then engineering test pilot Leo Sullivan at the controls. Veteran Art Hansen sat in the copilot's seat and Bob Brennan was strapped into the flight engineer's throne. Also on board were Lloyd Frisbee, Lockheed's chief development engineer; Ed Schockley, the company's lead flight test engineer; and Carroll Fruth, another flight engineer along to help out with various systems tests. It

Hercules will get the job done—one way or another—in this case, with a low altitude parachute extraction system (LAPES) delivery.

was the third flight of the airplane that was basically the same aircraft that had been delivered to Edwards just eight months earlier, but due to design and engineering advancements on the production line it was an even better machine. Leo and Herk had taken to each other immediately, but on this, their third flight together, Leo brought in the C-130 with his usual skill, unaware that fuel was streaming from behind the left inboard engine. During the roll-out, a fire erupted.

Now, if there is anything that gets a flight crew's immediate and undivided attention, it's an aircraft fire. Back in his observation seat in the aft cargo compartment, Fruth was the first to sight the fire; flames erupted from the number two engine as Leo used reverse pitch to slow the landing aircraft. Immediately, Fruth alerted the others ("Fire on number two engine! Fire in number two!"), and Shockley shouted from his flight deck seat, "Shut down number two . . . panic handle!" Leo was already in action, the increased adrenaline triggered by Fruth's voice on the intercom giving him almost superhuman reaction time. He shut down number two with the condition lever, pulled the emergency fire handle, and pushed the fire extinguisher button. Without a pause he did the same to number one, wheeled the careening Hercules sharply to the left off the runway onto the grass, and braked to a stop.

"Let's get the hell out of here!" shouted Sullivan, delaying his own exit until he, Hansen, and Brennan could secure the remaining two engines and turn off all aircraft power. True to the tradition of the air, he was the last to leave the burning C-130.

The fire equipment was already on the scene. After making sure that everyone was off the aircraft and while the fire fighters were still extinguishing the blaze, Leo ran back up to eyeball the damage and try to ascertain the cause. He retreated just as the burning wing collapsed.

The postfire investigation traced the cause of the fire to a quick-disconnect fuel line, and a firm engineering fix eliminated any future chance of such a malfunction. In an effort that was to be typical of the grand manner in which the Hercules could be repaired, even after such a serious wound, the Lockheed people mounted a new left wing and the aircraft returned to the air to carry out the remainder of the operational test program. The second production aircraft was programmed to be tested to destruction and was, ceasing to exist as other than a pile of metal by February 1957.

The remaining five development aircraft were redesignated JC-130As and flown to the Edwards and El Centro test centers, then to Eglin Air Force Base, and finally to the 4900th, 6401st, 6515th, and 6549th test squadrons before officially joining the Tactical Air Command. By September 1957, the first operational Hercules were flying overseas to join the 314th Tactical Air Wing (TAW) at Evreux-Fauville Air Base in northern France.

Indicative of the destined worldwide use of the Hercules, less than two years later Australia became the first foreign nation to add the C-130 to its military forces. It purchased an even dozen of the last of the A models.

And like us, they got a good buy! The *first* production aircraft is still flying today as a gunship AC-130A after an interim stint as a JC-130A missile tracker. Assigned to the Air Force Reserve's 711th SOS (Special Operations Squadron), it will have thirty-four birthday candles to

blow out on April 7, 1989, and you can bet your bottom buck it will be able to do so!

So, some former trash haulers are a little more venerable than others. They have included in their cargo all manner of ammunition and combat supplies, soldiers and marines, the famished and homeless human flotsam and jetsam of world disasters and indifference, hay for cattle in the snow-covered western U.S., vehicles of a thousand descriptions, penguins and seals from Antarctica, royalty, and the common people of fifty-eight nations. It was perhaps the saddest time

Cold weather operations are routine as MAC C-130s regularly participate in NATO exercises above the arctic circle in temperatures well into the minus numbers.

of all for the Hercules when it hauled the wounded and dead of Vietnam.

The C-130B, introduced in 1958, was a major model change in several respects. To begin with, Allison had developed the T56A-7 turboprop and added 300 eshp to the engine; this meant an

The troop-carrying capacity of the Hercules insures that the various firepower and assault teams arrive as complete units ready for combat.

increase of 1,200 eshp to the Hercules' already excellent power-to-weight ratio. A side-loading cargo door was installed just aft of the crew boarding door on the port side. Recognizing the crew fatigue factor (the Herk was flying longer and longer missions), a pair of bunks was installed across the aft bulkhead on the flight deck. Maximum ramp weight was increased from 124,200 pounds to 135,000 pounds. While the maximum payload went down slightly (35,000 to 34,840) a real gain was realized in fuel capacity, which went from 6,150 gallons in the A model to 6,960 gallons in the B, all carried internally in new bladder tanks. The A model had used two external wing-hung tanks for 900 gallons of its total. All B models incorporated the

stuck-out chin radome installed on the later A models. And, as with the A models, a number of modifications were made to the B models to produce rescue and weather aircraft, ECM (electronic countermeasures) platforms, gunships, ski versions, and so on. We'll talk about each of them later on.

The E models were next, coming on the scene in 1961. Major model changes included the omission of the forward cargo door that had been installed on the C-130Bs; it was discontinued after the first eight E models. The dash-7 Allisons were retained, but provisions were made to carry a pair of external fuel tanks under the wings, inboard of the outboard engines. Each carried 1,360 gallons of jet juice, resulting in a dramatic fuel load increase of 2,720 gallons, and the range of the C-130 increased. In addition, the payload for structural changes allowed an increase of 20,000 pounds in maximum gross weight. With the E model, the Hercules really hit its stride.

Finally, in 1974, Lockheed produced the H model, distinguished primarily by the more powerful Allison T56A-15 engine (which had already proven itself in earlier HC-130H rescue aircraft as far back as 1964). To the untrained eye, the H looked just like the E, although a minor difference was the elimination of hang racks for the rocket-assist takeoff units.

Currently, the C-130H-30 Super Hercules is being marketed. Its 30-foot fuselage stretch gives 1,557 cubic feet more of bulk cargo space over the basic L-100.

But for now, taking into consideration that we are looking at an aircraft basically unchanged in overall configuration for more than thirty-four years, just what is it that makes a Herk a Herk? What are the design features that give this remarkable aircraft its longevity and suitability for so many roles?

Interestingly enough, each of them can be found on one or more other aircraft; it's only on the Hercules that they are all bound together in what may be the closest thing to a perfect aircraft — for its tasks — that we will ever see.

Consider that stubby, jutted-out chin that gives the Hercules its singular appearance. What genius decided to install the radar at the bottom front of the fuselage rather than in the middle? No one, really. It's just that with the pilots sitting so far forward — for good combat visibility — the lower section of the nose is a natural place for the installation, and a personality is born!

How about combat visibility, something we have always considered in fighter design but hardly ever in transports? Why not? The Lockheed folks considered that factor as they planned for an aircraft that could very well have to taxi across pockmarked landing areas. It helped the pilots, too, if they could watch their drop zone drift closer. Hence, the great array of square and rectangular windows that surround the forward cockpit area. Big psychological advantage, also. It's nice to sit almost outdoors at 30,000 feet.

Take the big, boxy cargo space, which is the essence of the Hercules personality. The C-119 had one almost as big. The C-141 has one twice as large. But like the best of the three bears, the Hercules has one that is ''just right'' for an aircraft that must squeeze in and out of very restricted, rough fields.

And the space is quickly convertible. Want to carry paratroopers instead of cargo? Simply lower sling seats for seventy-six. Ground delivered troops? You can rerig for ninety-six in min-

The C-130E, with its increased range and load-carrying capacity, is the most prolific model of the Hercules series, each of its two underwing tanks providing 1,360 gallons of jet fuel.

utes — or sling litters to back-haul seventy-two wounded. Combinations of all of the above? Your dedicated loadmaster can handle that, too. And in extremis, when the requirements of combat dictate an override of normal seating, he's not above strapping a few souls to the upraised rear ramp. May be a bit uncomfortable, but it gets you into and out of hell when needed.

The ingenious on-load/off-load ramp design is efficient. Other aircraft have had clamshell doors — much more cumbersome and unable to be opened in flight. With the Herk you drop and deliver — or load.

The two paratrooper doors on each side of the after fuselage provide quick egress for the jumpers, a double stream of ready-to-fight tigers.

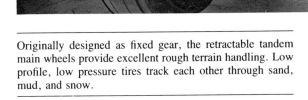

Not an inch of cargo space is wasted. It is not rare for cargo or troops going into combat to be strapped onto the lower cargo door. Note the two paratrooper exit doors on each side of the fuselage forward of the ramp.

Originally designed as fixed gear, the retractable tandem main wheels provide excellent rough terrain handling. Low profile, low pressure tires track each other through sand, mud, and snow.

The addition of the retractable windscreen makes their egress a bit less traumatic.

Look closely at the twin-tandem, low-profile, low-pressure tires, the front pair to break trail and the rear pair to follow on packed soil. Easy to fair in for less drag; easy to get to for quick service.

Inside the airplane, marvel at the spacious flight deck. The two pilots sit in splendor before their own array of instruments and dials, each able to duplicate the other's actions in all but a few functions. The flight engineer literally sits on a throne, albeit not a particularly regal one, behind, between, and slightly above the pilots. He has a commanding view of the whole cockpit area and is instantly available to either pilot should a question — or problem — arise. He keeps happy with his own array of dials, switches, and instruments, secure in the knowledge that he is an essential unit of the trio that operates the Hercules. One could argue that the navigator has a bit less space than in earlier aircraft, but hey! he doesn't need an elaborate chart table anymore. Sophisticated black boxes require only his input, monitoring, and reading to keep the aircraft within *feet* of its intended path over the earth. Finally, to add a bit of homey atmosphere that is most welcome on long flights, there are two thick-foam bunks (B model and some later configurations) and an ample minigalley to supply hot and cool liquids and provide for heating frozen dinners.

The pilots' "office" is designed for crew efficiency and comfort on long flights. Precedent-setting visibility impressed onlookers even at first rollout of the prototype. The small wheel to the left of the pilot's yoke is for nose wheel steering.

The overhead domain of the flight engineer features usage-designed controls and monitoring gauges.

One wag once said that flying a C-130 is something like sitting on your front porch and flying your house around. Well, any crew member worth his salt will argue that it is a pretty upper middle class dwelling — no cheap shotgun rental. Yes, sir, some aircraft have one or more of the same features that make the Herk a Herk, but only the Herk has them all.

Necessity, the perennial mother of invention, has caused the role of the Hercules to be expanded far beyond that of logistic airlift, yet that prime task has remained one of the major achievements of the C-130. Aficionados, impressed with the clattering sounds of alliteration, have constantly referred to it as the classic cargo carrier. And it indeed is. With its roll-on/roll-off capability,

it has hauled an almost infinite variety of objects, from palletized cargo to other aircraft. It hauls large containered objects that slide in its rear like some giant suppository, with only inches to spare. It hauls land vehicles, water vehicles, and ice vehicles. It hauls bulk liquids in a quickly installed cylindrical tank that holds 3,600 gallons, and the installation is so versatile that the contents of the tank either can be delivered somewhere or, if a suitable liquid, used to refuel other aircraft or feed the mother aircraft herself.

With its superb low-speed handling characteristics, its sturdy landing gear, and its rapid deceleration capability, it can deliver a maximum load onto a dirt strip that previously had been a challenge for an aircraft half its size. And it is just

The caterpillar becomes a butterfly as the Hercules soars skyward and "cleans up" by retracting its landing gear and flaps.

this capability that has given the Hercules one of its prime roles as a humanitarian.

That aspect of the multipersonality Hercules showed itself early on. In mid-September 1965, with open warfare breaking out between Pakistan and India, seven C-130s engaged in DEEP FURROW in Turkey were diverted to Iran and used to evacuate some 650 U.S. nationals.

Think for a moment of the summer of 1971. United States C-130s airlifted thousands of East Pakistanian war refugees into India's Assam Province at the request of the United Nations, some of the grateful people dropping to kiss the feet of the American crewmen.

Or consider the impact the Hercules made on the famished people of Nepal in 1972 when the C-130Ks of the RAF threaded their way down through six of the world's highest peaks, all over

26

26,000 feet, to deliver a cargo hold full of wheat onto a 3,100-foot dirt strip at Serkhet. The planes were followed over the next days by airdrops at remote locations, where flying down narrow, twisting valleys and dodging miles-high peaks were required on every flight.

Then there was the devastating earthquake (7.7 on the Richter scale) that struck a small village in the Davir Desert of Iran in 1978. There was nothing the Hercules could do for the 20,000 people killed when the earth shook, but almost immediately Iranian Air Force Hercules were on the scene, bringing in tons of medical supplies, tents, and food.

Wherever there has been a natural disaster — or a not-so-natural one — in all probability Hercules was there: Guam typhoon relief in 1976, Turkey earthquake relief the same year. Closer to home, in 1977, Hercules joined with big brothers C-141 and C-5 to airlift snow-handling equipment and relief personnel from Colorado, Iowa, Michigan, North Carolina, and New York into Niagara Falls, New York, for snow-cleanup operations.

It's almost an annual event, now, for Air National Guard (ANG) as well as regular and reserve MAC forces to show up over the plains states during the dead of winter to drop hay to starving cattle.

And a more recent example of Herk the Humanitarian at work took place in September 1987. Puerto Rican authorities became understandably alarmed at predictions of an outbreak of epidemic proportions of dengue hemorrhagic fever, a mosquito-spread disease that attacks the bones and is extremely painful. There is no known cure. Federal disease control authorities turned to the 907th Tactical Airlift Group, which maintains the only fixed-wing aerial spraying unit within MAC, the 356th Tactical Airlift Squadron. The USAFR (Reserve) aircraft deployed immediately to San Juan and started their low-level spraying operation. Flying at 150 feet, a necessarily low altitude to insure proper settlement of the chemical spray, the Hercules weaved among and around the tall buildings of San Juan, their antidisease mist reaching into every street and alley and nook and cranny where mosquitoes could be harbored. As evidence of their efficiency, a control group of 2,500 mosquitoes, set at various spots within the city and housed in escapeproof cages, was 99.8 percent eliminated.

The units of the 356th returned to their home base at Rickenbacker Air National Guard Base, Ohio, carrying with them the grateful acknowledgments of Puerto Rican authorities and the people of San Juan.

Logistic airlift — military and civilian — is the trademark of the Hercules. Even as you read this, chances are that the C-130s of the nations of the world are making their appointed rounds on all seven continents of our planet.

Chapter 3
Tactical Airlift

Ben Franklin had the right idea. After watching an unoccupied balloon rise into the clouds during an August 1783 visit to France, he mused, "Five thousand balloons, capable of raising two men each, could not cost more than five ships of the line; and where is the prince who could afford so to cover his country with troops for its defense as that 10,000 men descending from clouds might not in many places do an infinite deal of mischief before a force could be brought to repel them?" Old Ben liked long and somewhat confusing sentences in his musings, but his thoughts were certainly prophetic. The huge airdrops of World War II bore him out, although balloons had long been replaced by fixed-wing aircraft.

The use of airlift by the U.S. in a tactical situation was developed in the 1939–1945 worldwide conflict, sharpened to a specialized skill in the early 50s by our tasks in Korea, and honed to surgical precision by our long, costly involvement in Vietnam during the 60s and 70s. And

Shape of things to come: the stretched-fuselage C-130H-30 demonstrates its increased capability by airdropping a palletized Army "Goat" all-terrain vehicle.

the current surgeon wielding the precision airlift knife of the 80s is called Hercules.

One has only to speak with a veteran of Khe Sahn during the Tet Offensive. The ultimate test of the Hercules came there as well as to so many other places in Vietnam. Crews flew around the clock, through dangerously clear skies and in turbulent monsoon rain clouds, and bulled their way through ground fire to deliver the ammunition and other supplies vital to our troops' survival. The Hercules smashed onto the dirt with reversed props roaring their defiance at the surrounding enemy, off-loaded their precious cargos — often on the run — and blasted back into the air for more of the same.

When landings were too dangerous or impossible because of strip damage or enemy action, the Hercules roared down the strip and delivered their payloads by use of their low-altitude parachute-extraction system — LAPES. The pilot brought the Hercules down a steep descent, leveling off only a few feet above the dirt. At the predetermined point that the air delivery system (ADS) was activated, an extraction parachute streamed behind the aircraft. Three seconds later, the cargo was pulled from the aircraft; it dropped the short distance to the ground and slid violently to a stop — on target. The Hercules curled skyward, the loadmaster scrambling to belt himself down as the pilot took evasive action and the two-section cargo door closed.

A number of Hercules made only the first half of such a delivery, their sturdy bodies shattered by enemy fire and their mortally wounded crews trying to save their cargos even as their aluminum coffins slid burning across the dirt.

They died on the stop-and-go deliveries, too. A plump Herk, sitting helplessly while troops frantically off-loaded its cargo, was an irresistible target and drew Charlie's fire like a magnet attracts iron filings, thus its irreverent Nam designation as a "mortar magnet," an apt example of the grim humor of war.

Where there is no landing strip, the Hercules shifts to its PLAD (parachute low-altitude delivery system) mode. Approaching the drop zone, the pilot sets up his aircraft at 120 knots IAS with flaps down to give a level attitude and holds his altitude at 200 feet above the ground. The ADS is activated and the sequence of extraction places the load into a short, parachute-slowed drop. Properly executed, the drop causes the load to hit the target with little or no forward speed.

There is still another method of air delivery of cargo — the ground proximity extraction system (GPES). This is the most exact placement of air-delivered cargo, but it does require ground-based cargo-arresting equipment, which is basically a steel cable stretched across the extraction point. The cable is attached at both ends to a pair of "water twister" energy absorbers. At an indicated airspeed of 120 knots and an altitude of 5 feet, the pilot brings the Hercules across the cable, and the extended hook grabs the cable and the load is pulled from the aircraft.

Certainly, a hostile air or ground environment complicates the tasks of Hercules, yet the aircraft has shown remarkable stamina and strength in such an environment. The everyday pounding that is characteristic of combat flying — the radical maneuvers, steep climbs and descents, slamming onto the ground in assault landings, punishment of ill-prepared or battle-damaged airstrips, fast turnarounds, field maintenance — all are the meat and potatoes of Hercules' combat rations. Unbelievable damage from ground fire has been sustained and the C-130 has made it back, limping and bloody but needing only a few days to lick its wounds. But there are limits; the U.S. lost sixty-six Herks in Vietnam. Still, the C-130 shines in the role of combat delivery; Hercules is, first of all, a warrior, conceived for that singular purpose. It is in combat that the aircraft fulfills its prime destiny.

And it does so with a very versatile flair.

Hercules the Bomber

The beauty of fall foliage blanketing the state of Kentucky boggles the eye. Reds, rusts, oranges, yellows, browns, and September traces of lingering green provide a horizon-to-horizon palette of spectacular color. The thick foliage that covers the rolling hills of the home of good bourbon and fast thoroughbreds is preparing for winter. Far up in the northeast corner sits the hamlet of Argillite, and I swing off of Interstate 64 onto State Highway 1. At Argillite, I find the general store. Phoning for directions, I am instructed to take the access road just across from the store. It immediately becomes a winding gravel road that several miles later leads up a challenging hill to a red brick two-story home.

Inside, Sam McGowan leans back in his chair

beside the paneled wall of his den and smiles broadly.

I've come to talk Hercules with him.

Sam flies business jets now and is a company Citation (Cessna) pilot for Ashland Oil. Married and settled in his hideaway Kentucky home, Sam is typical of the thousands of Hercules crewmen who put their time in Nam and now are getting on with their lives. But those times are still in Sam's memories and he is working on a book about the development of tactical airlift during the Vietnam era. He talks animatedly about his research and breaks out some photographs he's received from the USAF repository in Washington, D.C. I thumb through them and my eyes stop on a shot of a Hercules cargo bay. Tied down to a pallet is a fat 10,000-pound bomb. I glance up at Sam and wait for his explanation, for my trip into the Kentucky backwoods has been solely for the purpose of talking to a rare individual, a C-130 bombardier.

Sam's eyes grow serious behind his glasses and he unconsciously reaches up and smooths his dark hair, as if the stroking will rekindle his memory. Apparently, it does.

Yes, I was one of a few — the only enlisted people in Vietnam with the authority to release bombs. The idea had been around for a while — the use of heavy bombs to blast out helicopter landing pads in the jungle. They tried dropping them by helicopter at first, from those Flying Cranes — CH-54s? — then some C-130 types heard about the project and suggested trying C-130 drops. We loaded them out of Cam Rahn Bay.

I had heard the stories. The USAF used the big 10,000-pound, and later the 15,000-pound, general-purpose bombs for clearing urgently

A welcome sight remembered by many a Vietnam ground-pounder—the Hercules penetrated SAM-infested skies and hostile ground fire to deliver critical supplies and ammo.

needed helicopter landing pads.

We rigged them to a modified drop system and their fuses were set to cause detonation at treetop height — that way, the blast wouldn't dig a crater, just clear out everything within a 100–200-foot radius. They really did the job. Some of the 10,000-pounders malfunctioned, however — they were old — and that's why they tried the 15,000-pounders.

I had read stories where the bombs were just rolled off the lowered loading ramp.

No way are you going to roll a 10,000-pound bomb off. We used our regular extraction system and conducted the drop pretty much like any other.

I had also heard stories about using them against personnel.

A Herk, nose-high in slow flight, disgorges combat-ready paratroopers.

No, except in a few isolated cases, and then more by the South Vietnamese than us. A 10,000-pounder is not an antipersonnel weapon. And a 15,000-pounder is just that much bigger.

I ask about his claim to be one of the only enlisted bombardiers.

Sam laughs. *True. Of course, I was actually a loadmaster. But, if you think about it, all the other folks releasing bombs were officers. B-52 crews, fighter attack pilots, navy pilots. All officers. But when we used the C-130 as a bomber, the loadmaster became the bombardier. I proba-bly dropped around a hundred bombs or so.*

Sam is twenty years beyond his Vietnam days and probably a pound or two heavier although still pilot trim. But as he talks, I can see how easily his mind slides back those two decades.

My first tour was in 67–68. Actually, I had been posted to France in 1965, but was diverted to Kadena [Okinawa] for Vietnam assignment. Oddly enough, when I got there, I didn't go straight into Vietnam operations. Instead, I found myself diverted from Kadena to take part in the Dominican Republic crisis but finally got back to Naha and flew my first Vietnam missions from there . . . logistic type runs. . . . At the end of my tour I wound up back at Pope AFB and participated in airdrops of army troops from First Cavalry prior to their deployment. . . . I found myself in the Philippines — Mactan — a post– World War II field that was hastily activated when the Vietnam thing started escalating. Tent city on a tiny island just to the east of central Cebu. I flew Vietnam missions from there and later Clark AFB. . . . We'd be in-country for a number of days, usually one day to fly over, fourteen days of operations with maybe one day off, then a day back to Clark for a rest — but that didn't always happen. When things were hot we'd hit Clark for maybe just forty-eight hours and then back to Nam. . . . During one stint, we flew twenty-four sorties in one fifteen-hour period.

Sam shakes his head as he recalls that one, later on commenting that it was a ninety-hour flight-time month, which is considerable when you're flying two- or two-and-a-half-hour sorties. He was flying A models and, along with all his crew, got a little groggy. After all, ninety hours of flight time means close to one hundred fifty to two hundred hours, when you consider briefings and preflight and postflight requirements and the additional stress of taking hostile fire. You find yourself doing your job almost automatically, as if in a daze, and that's when you make mistakes. On one occasion Sam exited the crew entrance hatch (on the forward left side of the fuselage) to open the exhaust doors for the ground turbine unit (GTU), which was housed in the left main gear housing. Proceeding aft, he inadvertently passed between the whirling propeller of the inboard engine and the fuselage. (Next time you see a Hercules turning up, take a look at the prop clearance.) Not a healthy move and Sam grins sheepishly as he recalls how he didn't even realize it until he was at the GTU door with his screwdriver.

My second tour, during 69–70, was a bit more interesting, if that's the right word. During my previous tour we flew mostly logistic missions, and hostile ground fire wasn't that bad, but during the second tour, activities were stepped up and we lost aircraft. I was involved in the Blind Bat operations, where we flew at night and acted

---

A 10,000-pound general purpose bomb is loaded into a Hercules "bomber" in Vietnam. Released over dense forest, the bomb exploded at treetop height, creating an instant helicopter operating pad.

Decoy flares erupt from a Hercules equipped with SATIN (survivability augmentation for transport installation), a system developed in 1987. Timed right, the hot projectiles lure away the deadly heat-seeking SAMs.

as a forward air control unit. . . . We carried flares and would illuminate for the F-4s and A-1s and the navy A-6s and A-4s. . . . That was an interesting operation.

Sam likes the adjective "interesting." I would probably have used scary, or hazardous, or even wild as hell.

We had a homemade flare chute — they fabricated them back at Naha out of sheet metal — that stuck out a partially opened ramp door. One of the loadmasters — and we usually carried three or four on flare missions — would have to load up to six flares and hold them manually until told to release. It wasn't easy and you would have to use your legs and feet at times and you'd get pretty tired waiting for the pilots to find a target to illuminate. I recall one incident where the loadmaster just couldn't hang on any longer and had to let go. . . . The pilot started to chew him out until the flares illuminated and there sat the very target we were looking for!

I think the bombing missions and the flare operations really showed how versatile the Hercules is.

You can see that Sam has only the fondest

memories of the ability of the C-130, but not all of his memories are good ones.

It's a rugged bird . . . we lost airplanes but not always the crew. The Herk could take a lot. And just because we were flying bombing or flare missions we didn't have to abandon our primary tasks of airlift. In fact, it was not unusual after a bombing mission to deliver a payload or back-load cargo or wounded. Often, that was the toughest part, loading the casualties and trying to keep them alive until you could get them to better medical facilities. On one occasion, I re-member the blood; the cargo deck was wet with it and after off-loading it was necessary to call a fire truck and hose it down. I did it myself, and I will never forget that: washing away the life's blood of our people with a fire hose.

For the next hour, we look at Sam's slides and photographs, discussing their use in his up-coming book. He seems to have almost total recall of the myriad of details that stay with you after a combat tour — even one twenty years back. As an afterthought, he adds a final detail to the bombing missions.

We had a very small circular error in our drops, something less than thirty yards as I recall, and from 7,000 feet that's good. I was told we had the most accurate bombing record in Nam at the time, although I don't recall what the criteria was. We'd just set the bomb in a cradle on a cargo pallet and secure it with nylon webbing straps. At the one-minute warning, we'd untie all except the right-hand locks and stream the drogue chute. There was a sharp knife incorpo-rated in the release system and our headphones had been modified to hear ground transmissions. . . . We'd get release instructions from the ground — five-four-three-two-one-hack! — and

we'd pull the release and out the bomb would go. There were no letdown chutes, just the drogue to pull it out and stabilize it. It would fall straight down.

The interview is over. I have a ways yet to travel this day and Sam has his own book to work on. It'll be a good one. We linger for a moment in the backyard, exchanging small talk and thanking each other for our mutual interest in the Hercules. As I turn my car around in his driveway, Sam waves good-bye. Sam, the Hercu-les bombardier — now Sam, the corporate pilot.

Airlift Rodeo

Tactical airlift is certainly not an American exclu-sive; every nation in the world that boasts an air force has some tactical airlift capability. For the major powers it is considerable, for the minor powers it is most probably barely adequate, for the others it is a luxury that can be afforded only by the use of aircraft not really designed for such a task.

Pope Air Force Base in North Carolina, the home of the 317th Tactical Airlift Wing, boasts the title of U.S. Airlift Center. The 317th has an illustrious history to justify its assignment to Pope. First activated in 1942 as the 317th Trans-portation Group and almost immediately redesig-nated the 317th Troop Carrier Group (TCG), the Group executed the first airborne operation in the southwest Pacific and eventually wound up on Leyte in 1944, supporting allied ground forces.

The 317th flew in the Berlin airlift and carried out a number of military and humanitarian opera-tions over the next four decades with only a

Spirited air delivery competition at the annual Airlift Rodeo held at Pope AFB produces a healthy byproduct: increased proficiency and combat readiness. Hercules crews from all over the world compete.

short pause for deactivation during 1959–1962.

Reorganized and stationed successively in France and Ohio, the 317th provided rotational assignments to Evreux-Fauville Air Base, RAF Mildenhall, the Canal Zone, and Germany. Down through the years the 317th flew such diverse missions as coverage for the manned space program and disaster relief in Yugoslavia, Libya, South and Central America, Cyprus, Chile, and our own hurricane-devastated Mississippi and Louisiana Gulf coasts. The 317th was among the airlift delivering troops to the Dominican Republic during the 1965 governmental crisis. In 1971, now designated a Tactical Airlift Wing (TAW), the 317th moved to Pope.

Annually since 1979, the 317th has acted as the host wing for Headquarters, Military Airlift Command (MAC) at Pope, for the conduct of the largest peacetime tactical airlift competition, Airlift Rodeo. Participants include tactical airlift units from a number of free world air forces that fly the C-130. Airlift Rodeo 87, for example, included squadrons from eleven foreign countries as well as nineteen home teams in the C-130 unit category (Airlift Rodeo also includes C-141, C-123, C-7, and individual flying and nonflying competition). Activities concentrate on specific tactical airlift tasks and competitors are graded to arrive at a comparison of performance. For all of its serious nature, it is a festive occasion, and there is a great deal of pride exhibited along with superb performance.

The winners in each event are indeed the best of the best in the airlift community and dear ole Uncle Sam has to fight quite hard to capture first place in any event. As a case in point, West Germany's 62d Air Transport Wing took top honors in the 1987 competition. Foreign winners in past years have included the United Kingdom (best Allied crew, three years running: 1980, 1981, 1982); Italy (best overall wing, 1982 and 1984); Germany (best C-130 maintenance: 1982, 1984); Australia (best foreign aircrew: 1983, 1985); New Zealand (best C-130 aircrew: 1984); and Portugal (best C-130 aircrew, best short-field landing, best foreign aircrew: 1986). In 1987, competitors included units from Australia, Brazil, Canada, Germany, Italy, Israel, Morocco, Portugal, and the United Kingdom.

Although intensely competitive, techniques are observed, procedures are discussed, and overall mission conduct is examined with the end result that everyone goes away with a new appreciation for the demanding tasks of C-130 tactical airlift. The star of the whole show, of course, is the Hercules, and there is continual fascination with the skill with which the ole girl is put through her paces. Spot landings rival the precision of air show performances; delivery events are a professional potpourri of everything from airdrops of troops and cargo to LAPES and PLAD events. Such concentration, even for international competitive purposes, has a valuable effect on tactical airlift ability, because units and crews compete to attend and compete to win at Pope, and in that intense competition, actual combat prowess is honed to a fine edge. Then when the time comes for the real thing, the efforts at Airlift Rodeo, along with the year-round training, pay off handsomely.

Hercules in Grenada

In October 1983, when the United States answered the call of the Organization of the Eastern

A tired Hercules grabs a rest after the 1983 Grenada invasion. AC-130 gunships were in the forefront of the successful assault and rescue of U.S. nationals.

Caribbean States to join their Caribbean Peace-keeping Forces in restoring the government of Grenada to a democratic and stable state, we began the first large-scale, multiservice combat use of air power since Vietnam. Operation UR-GENT FURY, the invasion of Grenada, was a textbook demonstration of the versatility of the Hercules as a war machine, because during that operation the vast majority of forces were delivered by air, primarily by C-130s.

The U.S. Air Force pulled together three MAC C-130 wings, the 314th out of Little Rock Air Force Base, the 317th out of Pope Air Force Base in North Carolina, and the 459th out of Andrews Air Force Base in Maryland. To them, the USAF added a C-130H wing, the 463d out of Dyess Air Force Base in Texas; the 1st Special Operations Wing (1st SOW) out of Hurlburt Field in Florida; a Reserve Tactical Airlift Group of C-130Es out of Willow Grove Naval Air Station

Fill 'er up and check the oil! A Special Operations HC-130H, its Fulton personnel recovery system arms folded back along its nose, tops off from a ready tanker before heading into hostile territory.

in Pennsylvania; and an Air National Guard unit, the 193d Electronic Combat Group, out of Harrisburg, Pennsylvania, who flew their sophisticated EC-130E Coronet Solo II psyops aircraft.

There were, of course, other fixed-wing airlift aircraft, such as the C-141 Starlifters and the C-5 Galaxies and the Navy's airevac C-9s (and the marines added their own assault lift helicopters), but it was the Hercules that was quite simply everywhere in the URGENT FURY airlift effort.

The first U.S. aircraft over Grenada on the morning of D day (October 24, 1983) was an AC-130H Spectre gunship (see Chapter 4) of the 1st SOW (one of its sister gunships would remain on station for more than sixteen hours, refueling three times from a KC-10 tanker operated by the 2d Bomb Wing).

Prior to the assault, the Spectre made a low-altitude reconnaissance over the long Cuban-built airstrip at Point Salines, and using low-level television and an array of infrared and electronic sensors determined that one third of the runway was obstructed by construction equipment and vehicles.

The first wave of ground troops, the 1st Ranger Battalion of the 75th Infantry Division, was airdropped by two MC-130E gunships and five troop-carrier C-130Es. The second wave, the 2d Ranger Battalion, followed on five additional C-130Es. The assault was made on the Point Salines area while the marines simultaneously executed their helicopter assault near the old airport at Pearls.

In the forefront of the assault, AC-130 gunships and MC-130H Combat Talon aircraft provided air support wherever needed, notably against the Cuban construction workers barracks at Point Salines when the Cubans attempted to turn the area into a stronghold.

As the operation progressed, the Hercules continued their support and resupply missions, including shuttles to Barbados to relay troops brought in by the Starlifters. The airstrip at Point Salines was still partially blocked and the reduced available length presented a problem for the heavier and faster C-141s; besides, the taxi area could handle only one of the large jet transports and the scarcity of unloading vehicles made the turnaround time for the Starlifters too risky. The C-130s were right at home in the restricted environment. They expanded their shuttle resupply flights to include Puerto Rico and the U.S. mainland.

The EC-130E Coronet Solo II conducted psyops operations over Grenada, broadcasting prerecorded tapes over its powerful loudspeaker system and relaying low-level radio programs.

As the operation neared termination, some of the AC-130s even took on SAR (search and rescue) duties. The first contingent of Cubans, along with five Red Cross escorts, boarded USAF C-130s and were ferried to Grantly Adams Airport at Barbados, where they transferred to a Cuban airlift for their return to Havana.

An interesting footnote: the United States Coast Guard Air Station at Clearwater, Florida, added two of their HC-130Hs to the operation, performing valuable SAR duties and also flying equipment resupply flights.

URGENT FURY, like its bloody predecessor, Vietnam, was a real demonstration of the varied roles we've given the mighty Hercules.

Maybe Zeus was not the only lover of the lady Alcmene. Perhaps she and Mars had a thing going — and Zeus just thought Hercules was his son. . . .

Chapter 4
Special Operations

Dirty, unshaven, fatigued almost to the point of collapse, the man makes his way through the predawn darkness to a small jungle clearing only seven miles inland from the spacious white sand beaches bordering the western Caribbean. By contrast, the circular clearing within the dense tropical forest is only twenty-five yards across and the trees around it reach up fifty or sixty feet. But it will do.

He forages around under the trees, finally scraping away the top of a prominent mound of humus, and pulls away a large canvas bag. He drags it to the center of the clearing and lays out the contents: a folded blimp-shaped balloon, several helium modules, a harness suit, and a length of nylon line wrapped around a canister. He glances at the sky and notes with some anxiety the first bleeding rays of the rising sun. He must hurry. Laying aside a small packet of miscellaneous items, he pulls on the harness suit and adjusts its chest and leg straps tightly against his body. Spreading out the balloon, he

fastens the line, making sure that it is free to uncoil, and double-checks its connections to his harness. Next, he joins the first helium module to the balloon and opens the pressure valve. The balloon begins to swell and within a few minutes it is a fully inflated miniblimp 24 feet long and 6 feet in diameter. He lets it rise. Gratefully, he notes that there is little wind and as the balloon reaches the 525-foot limit of the line, it hovers almost directly overhead.

Thirty miles out over the blue waters of the Caribbean, the thick, dark shape of a MC-130H Combat Talon Hercules hugs the waves as it speeds toward the coast. Inside, its ever-tracking INS (inertia navigational system) guidance system is taking it precisely from one predetermined checkpoint to another. Several of its crewmen are monitoring sophisticated electronic and infrared sensing devices. The two pilots are utilizing a much older and equally important sensor: the Mark I eyeball. They are approaching hostile territory and within minutes they will be moving through an unfriendly air and ground environment — with no defensive armament on board. Surprise, speed, and airman skill are their only weapons.

The Special Operations Hercules holds steady at its 150-foot height above the water. There is

---

A Pave Spectre AC-130H gunship leans into a firing bank, its sophisticated radar, TV, and infrared sensors searching for suitable ground targets.

a good chance that it is under any inquisitive radar lobe. But you never know. Ahead, just emerging in the dim dawn, is the coastal crossing checkpoint. The black-painted recovery aircraft eases up to 400 feet; the pilots need a bit more visibility to pick up the balloon. The radio homing beacon and their radar signal indicate their quarry is dead ahead.

There it is, its glossy sides reflecting the first morning rays. The MC-130H fine-tunes its altitude and from the sides of its irregular blunt nose housing two arms fold forward and form a large V. With unerring accuracy, the pilot aims the charging Hercules at the space just under the balloon. Back in the cargo compartment, the two recovery crewmen are strapped into their positions on the lowered loading ramp.

Contact! The balloon line is caught by the inside of the left arm and is guided to the center catch mechanism, which locks on it with an unbreakable grip.

Down below, the man feels the instantaneous jerk as he is pulled violently upward — straight upward. The amazing geometry of his sudden lift toward the sky provides a parabolic path that first carries him free of the forest trees, then streams him out behind the Hercules in an ever-climbing arc until his lifeline can be snagged and he is winched aboard the loading ramp. Aided by the Hercules crewmen, he scrambles forward and unbuckles his harness. Grinning, one of the loadmasters hands him a very cold beer as the ramp closes and the Hercules banks steeply back toward open water. Once again over international waters, the Combat Talon Hercules rendezvouses with a pair of MH-53H Pave Low helicopters (Sikorsky twin-turbined, single-rotor, heavy-lift choppers). From refueling pods on each wing,

just outboard of the engines, the Hercules streams a pair of refueling baskets. The MH-53Hs are very thirsty, having been about their own clandestine business. They plunge their open beaks into the baskets like hungry chicks in a nest and the linked trio sets its course for the Florida Panhandle.

Special Operations is in a class by itself. Tasks include unconventional warfare, psychological operations, foreign internal defense, and just about any operation that can't be conveniently typecast under normal operations. The air arm of Special Operations can trace its lineage back to a small group of air commandos in World War II, led by the legendary Col. Phillip G. Cochran. Commander of the 1st Air Commando Group, Cochran counted in his inventory C-47 transports, P-51 fighters, B-25 bombers, UC-64 utility aircraft, L-1 and L-5 observation airplanes, and CG-4A and TG-5 gliders. Ultimately his force operated in direct support of General Wingate's Burma invasion (British Brigadier Orde Wingate had long conducted behind-the-lines forays in enemy-occupied Burma and was an early Allied Special Operations commander).

Demobilized after WW II, Special Operations air forces were resurrected in 1950 as Air Supply and Communication Wings and assigned to the Military Air Transport Service. A series of administrative and operational evolutions followed, along with an increase in mission assignments, which included behind-the-lines rescue of downed pilots. An array of mixed aircraft found their way into the Special Operations inventory. Counterinsurgency entered the military vocabulary, and special air operations took on even more unconventional tasks. By the time Vietnam was in full swing with predominantly jet air power, Special Operations still carried out its varied assignments with T-28s, B-26s, A-1s, C-47s, and whatever other air machines they could get their hands on. Aerial propaganda broadcasts were made and Bullshit Bombers (C-47s and U-10s) showered enemy forces with propaganda and surrender leaflets. It was from the Vietnam requirements that two magnificent C-130 weapons evolved: the Spectre gunships and the Combat Talon assault transport aircraft.

Gunships and Special Operations

In American folklore, one of the heroes of the Old West was the gunslinger. Often elected town marshall, the skilled sharpshooter with the lightning-speed draw and deadly aim could pump out a devastating stream of lead. No wonder,

Crewmembers of a Special Operations Herk reel in their catch, a grateful behind-the-lines operative who has just experienced the wildest ride on earth.

then, that Hercules in one of its roles would become the airborne modern-day counterpart of the tall, straight-backed man in the white hat. And true to the early west image, the Hercules gunfighter can be a deadly enforcer of the law.

It may be that the gunship concept started with an innovative Army Air Corps type by the name of "Pappy" Gunn (what else?). In 1943, Maj. Paul T. Gunn rearmed some of his Douglas A-20 Havocs by installing an array of four .50-caliber machine guns in the nose of the light attack bomber. While an impressive modification, the four guns were not quite adequate for his purposes, and to install more would seriously threaten the CG (center of gravity) of the relatively small bomber. He needed a larger, heavier airplane and the B-25 just happened to be available. So Pappy not only slung four in the B-25's nose (eliminating the bombardier's position as he had in the A-20) but added a pair of saddlebag .50s on each side and a trio on the bottom just aft of the nose gear doors. Now, eleven .50s, all bore sighted, can throw out a formidable amount of lead. In March 1943 during the battle of the Bismark Sea, Pappy's A-20s and B-25s sank an entire Japanese convoy of twelve merchantmen and their escorting cruisers and destroyers. That, friends, is airborne firepower! The gunship concept had arrived.

The Korean fracas pointed up another aerial need — night interdiction. And the newly created

Left: Liverwurst or bratwurst? Two Special Operations sausages prepare to team up for a low-level personnel recovery task. *Right:* Teamwork is never an overused word in Special Operations, especially in this linkup of a HC-130H with its KC-135 tanker.

Go ahead—draw! With a devastating rate of fire that produces a near-solid stream of projectiles, the Hercules gunslinger rightly proclaims itself the best in the West.

Air Force came up with an ingenious method of providing that — Shoran — short-range navigational radar. With two radar beams crisscrossed over a target, the attacking aircraft would ride one beam to the intersection of the other and drop its bombs. So the second feature of a successful gunship concept, night interdiction (the first being ample firepower), was accomplished and the door was opened for further development.

The Vietnam conflict led to complete gunship development. The Special Air Warfare/Air Com-

mando Forces were noted for their unconventional solutions to battlefield problems. One difficulty facing them was a need for night close air support. The venerable C-47 was doing yeoman duty as a night illuminator and had a reasonable loiter capability. Captain Ronald W. Terry,

USAF, thus reasoned that the ancient Skytrain might be modified to give something more — airborne firepower support to the forces below. Under his guidance, several concepts were tried. One involved the installation of ten .30-caliber machine guns protruding through passenger windows and the cargo door! The final configuration found three 7.62mm GAU2B/A miniguns installed in the port side of the aircraft cargo compartment. The pilot utilized a standard Mark 20 Mod 4 gunsight mounted in his side window.

Thus, the AC-47 gunships were born. The concept was then tried in C-119 aircraft — with limited success. It was obvious that for the concept to reach its full potential, a faster, longer-legged and longer-winded, more modern vehicle was needed. And waiting in the wings like an ever-present understudy was the C-130.

Targets can run but not hide from this LLLTV (low level light television) and laser rangefinder platform installed in an AC-130.

Gunship ammo handlers face yet another exacting task upon return to base—they will have to shovel out the thousands of empty cartridge cases. Three-thousand rounds a minute mean a lot of empty brass.

As a gunship, the Hercules was to become a natural. Rugged, maneuverable, roomy (for gun installations and control consoles), and with staying power, the Hercules was an obvious follow-on to the earlier C-47 conversions. The classic Douglas Skytrain, known first as Puff (from its full Puff the Magic Dragon moniker) and later Spooky (from its sudden and deadly rain of death from night skies), had established the early tactics of gunship usage. They only needed to be adapted to the Hercules.

The first AC-130 gunships, called Fabulous Four-engined Fighters by admiring F-4 crews, were initially lightly armed and possessed a passable night-observation capability. But in the years to follow, there would be a series of progressive developments that would ultimately make the C-130 Spectre gunship series the most heavily armed aircraft in history (with respect to gunfire capability). Along with the conversion came expanded roles, including day and night FAC (forward air control), armed reconnaissance, and close air support; flareship; laser illuminator; sensor relay station; and even tank killer. The Gunship II program followed, the AC-130s being further modified to carry four 7.62mm GE MXU-470 minigun modules and four 20mm GE M61 Gatling cannons, all arranged on the left side of the fuselage, a pair of each forward of the left main gear pod and a pair of each aft. A NOD (night observation device) or a Starlight Scope along with a 20-kw searchlight gave each gunship a twenty-four-hour capability. A crude breadboard computer was utilized to solve windage problems.

Tactics involved circling counterclockwise around a selected target, holding an altitude just beyond ground-fire range, and adjusting the circle to compensate for wind drift. Fire was thus concentrated at a constant point on the surface. And

If all else fails, break out the biggies! A 40mm Bofors cannon and 105mm howitzer assault can spell hell on earth to anyone on the receiving end.

a deadly concentration it was!

With the deployment of the first AC-130 to Vietnam in September 1967, it became immediately apparent that Super Spooky, as the Herk was initially dubbed, was a potent weapon indeed, so much so, that the decision was made to convert nine more Hercules to the gunship role.

Overall, C-130s were in short supply, so it was necessary to use the older JC-130s (missile-tracking Hercules used to track missiles from Cape Canaveral). The first conversions were completed in June 1968 and deployed to Vietnam that December. Designated AC-130As, the gunships carried the same armaments package but were equipped with a more sophisticated sensor package — a Texas Instruments forward-looking infrared radar (FLIR), a Singer-General Precision fire-control computer, and a Texas Instruments moving-target indicator radar (MTI). By May 1969, nine AC-130s were operating out of the Ubon Thai Air Force Base.

Later on, twin 40mm Bofors cannons replaced the aft pair of 20mm Gatling cannons. A GE ASQ-145 low-light-level television (LLLTV) camera was added along with a beacon-tracking side-viewing radar. A video bomb damage assessor (BDA) was tied into the LLLTV, a new digital fire-control computer was installed, and a Korad AVQ-18 laser designator/range finder was added. In rapid order, a Pave Pronto configuration was reached by adding a Black Crow device, which could pick up spurious radiation signals from unshielded truck ignition systems. Finally came the Pave Spectre series of C-130 gunships — converted E and H models. The more powerful engines enabled the Hercules to carry more armor plate. Increased fuel capacity meant longer on-station time. Back in the cargo compartment,

the FLIR, LLLTV, electronic warfare, and Black Crow consoles and operators were grouped together in a compact compartment. Hercules was becoming a very aggressive warrior. One of the most welcome changes was a large observation bubble installed over a hole in the closed cargo door. Previously, the cargo door had been left lowered so that the illumination operator (IO) could hang over the lip and watch for incoming AAA or SAMs. Tethered to the deck, the crewman nevertheless could be thrown out during extreme evasive maneuvers and would have to be manually retrieved!

The Pave Spectre Hercules arrived at Ubon in December 1971. With the advent of SAMs, however, and more capable enemy ground fire, it was necessary to operate at higher and higher altitudes. A longer-ranged weapon was needed. The 40mms in the rear were replaced with army 105mm howitzers, which were equipped with flash suppressors and could fire a forty-two-pound shell four to five times a minute!

In 1972, the USAF decided to upgrade all C-130Es with dash-15 Allisons and an advanced avionics package. The AC-130Es subsequently became AC-130Hs, with the first four arriving at Ubon in March 1973.

From their inception, Spectre gunships were involved in practically every major operation in Vietnam, despite the eventual use by the VC and North Vietnamese of the Soviet SA-7 Stellar shoulder-fired missiles.

Special Operations had a permanent and very lethal weapon.

Today, the AC-130H Spectre gunships are currently assigned to the 16th Special Operations Squadron of the 1st Special Operations Wing at Hurlburt Field in Florida. The MAC command is the only active-duty operator of the H-model gunships. Companion AC-130A gunships are based at nearby Duke Field and assigned to the 919th Special Operations Group, Air Force Reserve. And the grand old gal of the entire world-wide Hercules fleet, C-130A Number 53-3129, the very first Marietta-produced Hercules and the same one that Leo Sullivan and his crew egressed from after their wing fire on April 15, 1955 (see Chapter 2), is now one of these AC-130As of the 919th and proudly bears the name THE FIRST LADY on its nose.

Along with the development of Herk the Gun-slinger came the development of the Combat Talon. The concept envisioned a penetrator that could inject Special Forces behind hostile lines and extract them when the time came. Such an aircraft should also be able to resupply clandestine forces and support covert operations. Also, it would be tactically advantageous to be able to refuel accompanying aircraft such as helicopters.

The excellent short unprepared field performance gave the Hercules part of that capability. Give it a reasonably long, flat spot and it could ground deliver or airdrop anything (within reason) or anybody. Equip it with an in-flight refueling system (the boom receptacle is on top of the fuselage just aft of the overhead cockpit windows) and in turn hang refueling pods on the outboard portion of each wing to service companion fixed- or rotary-wing aircraft and you would have a formidable long-legged Special Operations team. The ample flight deck and cargo compartment could accommodate an impressive array of sensor and guidance systems. Throw in a sophisticated electronic countermeasures (ECM) package and a terrain-following radar and you begin to have a very flexible air asset.

As for retrieval of personnel, there was the Fulton surface to air recovery (STAR) system.

The ever-ready ground armament crew takes over while the flight crew gets briefed for their next mission.

With a nose modification to mount the retractable trapping arms of the Fulton system yoke, and a retrieval winch back in the cargo compartment, the Hercules could swoop in on a lifeline held aloft by a helium-filled balloon and literally snatch a person from the bowels of enemy territory. Provisions were even made for a simultaneous two-man recovery, particularly valuable should a pararescue trooper have to jump and assist an injured comrade.

The Combat Talon Hercules has become a mainstay of the air arm of Special Operations, and crews maintain their STAR proficiency with regular snatches of 250-pound dummy loads (and welcome volunteers who might want one of the wildest rides on the midway). Current Combat Talon aircrews (six officers and five enlisted per crew) are trained in MC-130Es by the 8th Special Operations Squadron of the 1st Special Operations Wing at Hurlburt Field in Florida.

Just as Herk reached its peak as a fighting machine in the Spectre, it is the ultimate assault transport in its Combat Talon configuration.

Chapter 5
Aerospace Rescue and Weather Reconnaissance

The 55th Aerospace Rescue and Recovery Squadron (ARRS) sits over in a quiet spot on the Eglin Air Force Base flight line. As one of six squadrons assigned to the 39th Aerospace Rescue and Recovery Wing, the 55th boasts quite an illustrious history. In addition to its combat-related tasks, the squadron participated in numerous humanitarian missions, including the recovery of 900 bodies from the infamous People's Temple mass suicide at Jonestown, Guyana, in 1978. It was also deployed to Turkey in 1979 for the evacuation of U.S. citizens after the fall of the Shah of Iran.

I notice several of the squadron's HC-130s as I am led to the hangar by my escort, Capt. Sean Maynard, USAF. Once inside, Maynard gives me a brief but excellent rundown on squadron operations. He's enthusiastic about the Hercules and proud of the primary role of the 55th (worldwide search for location and recovery of aerospace personnel) and his contribution as a Herk driver.

A skillfully flown HC-130P of the 41st Rescue and Weather Reconnaissance Wing delivers a pair of rescue personnel to assist a downed airman.

We concentrate on low-level recovery in concert with our choppers. . . . Actually the rescue part of our mission is downplayed somewhat as we get more into the recovery business.

I thought that was the purview of the Special Operations folks. Could there be a duplication of missions here?

Not really . . . although we do, in a sense, operate much along the same lines. . . . Some folks say we're like "soft Special Ops," but that's more of a misnomer, really.

Then he grins.

Half the equipment; twice the skill.

Whatever the relationship, I can see that some of the tasks, tactics, and capabilities are similar.

Our aircraft have two 10,000-pound-capacity Benson internal fuel tanks and we can refuel two choppers at a time, a typical transfer being perhaps 5,000 pounds per chopper. We can operate up to a 1,800-mile radius. We carry two pararescue troops also when required.

I wonder about night operations.

Certainly. We have night-vision goggles and fly low level . . . the navigator doesn't need to look out. Have you ever looked through NVGs?

No, I'm forced to reply. My Hercules experience doesn't include the low-level terrain-following tactics these folks employ. The mere thought of winding through unfamiliar mountain valleys and passes at close to 300 knots with no moon and unseen tiny electrons in a terrain-following radar system telling me when to zig, zag, climb, and dive causes little knots to bounce around in my stomach. These people do it routinely. Maynard checks out a key and opens the night-vision equipment locker and takes out a pair of NVGs. He leads me to the ladies' room. Ladies' room? Grinning, he knocks. No answer, so we enter under the curious stares of a couple of his fellow pilots and he shuts the door.

This is the darkest place around . . . we use it for fitting and checking the goggles.

He hands me the pair and I hold them up to my eyes. In the mirror I look like a chameleon; the black eyepieces stick out several inches. I hand them back and Maynard makes sure a protective cover is in place and installs batteries. Then he flicks off the light to show me how dark it is in the little girls' room. I can see absolutely nothing. He helps me put on the goggles and I adjust the headband for a comfortable fit. They weigh a bit and I can imagine the load under the stresses of rough air and maneuvering. Maynard has me remove the protective covers. Voila! I can see Maynard, the sink, the faucets, the mirror, the stalls, the walls, the whole room. Not like daylight of course, but in varying shades of gray. I could navigate around the ladies' room. And I can see how one could fly by visual reference, even on the darkest night — but I'm not anxious to try it. Impressive, and these are the older models.

Later on we take a look at one of the Sikorsky UH-60A assault helicopters. The Blackhawk is a lean, mean machine and I have no trouble imagining it as a worthy partner with the Hercules in the Aerospace Rescue and Recovery business. Then, we look over one of the squadron Herks and I note with interest the installation of the two internal Benson tanks and the aerial refueling system. The Hercules looks very businesslike, squatting there. I must have seen a thousand C-130s since I became an aficionado, and yet each time I approach one I am filled with that same feeling of admiration and respect for the machine. In my mind's eye, I envision this one skimming the dark surface of unfamiliar terrain, the flight deck crew silent and serious as they peer outside through the chameleon goggles and at the same time monitor the aircraft's systems that make such penetration possible. Not much room for error. Like maybe none.

There is a distinct similarity between the H models the 55th flies and the Combat Talon of the Special Operations squadrons, but there is no STAR recovery system. The squared-off nose radome is still present on most ARRS Herks, however, and their early makeup included the recovery yoke.

Maynard points out the dual tracks that are positioned on the overhead of the cargo compartment, then explains the exterior dual tracks on the upper cargo door. It's all part of the ODS (overhead delivery system), which was original equipment on the first HC-130Hs. (Incidentally, those early ARRS aircraft had the dash-15 engines a few years before the standard C-130H appeared with them as a normal installation.) When you open the cargo doors, the upper rises to bring its tracks level and in line with the cargo compartment tracks. The ODS was designed to facilitate the loading, unloading, and delivery of air rescue kits, and in the original concept they could also be used, with the aid of an inter-

The Aerospace Rescue and Recovery team, a lead HC-130P and its companion UH-60A Blackbird helicopter, shares body fluids en route to hostile territory.

valometer, to precision drop a series of life rafts for water rescue. But I gather from further comments that the system offers no real advantage over the more common container delivery system (CDS), and the rails will probably be removed.

A typical long-range rescue mission would involve filling both the internal tanks as well as the external, and augmenting the crew to thirteen personnel. At a weight of more than 173,000 pounds (86,320 pounds of fuel on board), the rescue Herk could proceed outbound for a distance of 2,500 statute miles, search at wave-top height for almost three hours, complete its Fulton recovery (with up to three passes), and return to base with ample reserves. Typical flight time would be in excess of eighteen hours. For night operations, the HC-130H carried ten flare tubes, and for situations where the Fulton system could not be employed, four to six six-man rafts.

During the first years of Hercules ARRS service, several HC-130s were modified to become HC-130Ns (addition of advanced direction-finding gear and a retrieval system for recovering space capsules) or HC-130Ps, with a primary mission of refueling helicopters. Later on, the refueling capability would be almost a standard feature of ARRS C-130s.

Weather reconnaissance Hercules out of Keesler AFB, Mississippi, regularly locate and track Gulf and Caribbean storm cells and hurricanes, a wing-flexing task that has earned them their moniker, Storm Trackers.

WRS

There is an early tie-in between the Aerospace Rescue and Recovery Service and the Weather Reconnaissance Service (WRS). The latter mission (in C-130s) began in 1964 with the Air Force purchase of five brand-new WC-130Bs and the designation of the commands as the Rescue and Weather Reconnaissance Wings of the Aerospace and Rescue Recovery Service (which in turn was under the operational command of the Military Air Transport Service, but we're not

here to get lost in the complex command channels of the military, so we will keep such discussions to a minimum). Later on the weather Herks were transferred to the Tactical Air Command and finally to the Military Airlift Command, where all Hercules are today.

Despite that early association and a slight overlapping of tasking, the weather Herks have come into their own as integral assets of the Air Force and in so doing have become a valuable adjunct to the National Weather Service as well. There is also a single, civilian-operated U.S. National Oceanic and Atmospheric Administration (NOAA) Hercules, which is tied into the overall monitoring of global weather.

The mission of the weather Herks is worldwide indeed, with specific tasks including weather patrols in areas of possible combat and advance weather surveillance along long-range over-water routes to be flown by fighter and attack aircraft.

Perhaps one of the most valuable tasks, however, concerns the investigation and tracking of seasonal weather phenomena such as typhoons and hurricanes.

The 815th Weather Reconnaissance Squadron, aptly named the "Storm Trackers" and based at Keesler Air Force Base in Biloxi, Mississippi, is an Air Force Reserve squadron and one of fourteen subordinate units assigned to the 403d Rescue and Weather Reconnaissance Wing (RWRW). As squadrons go, the 815th is relatively small: forty-four officers and twenty-four airmen, including ten officers and ten airmen who are Air Reserve technicians (ART, see Chapter 8). The unit employs four civilians.

It is late October when I am ushered into the squadron briefing room and meet with Maj. Gail

The calm before the storm—literally. AFRES pilots of the 815th WRS (Weather Reconnaissance Squadron) discuss penetration tactics en route to a reported storm position.

Carter, a squadron meteorologist, and Lt. Col. Ken Gates, a twelve-year Hercules driver and an ex–B-52 jock. Our small talk soon reveals that Gates has about as much time flying into (and out of, which is the other very vital half of the equation) hurricanes as I have total time in the Hercules. Major Carter gives me the hurricane briefing. We all know what hurricanes are, but a crewman on a hurricane-penetration flight needs to have a bit more detailed knowledge of the makeup and ferocity of one of nature's largest destructive whirlwinds.

The 815th has global responsibilities that take its planes and crews well beyond the immediate area of the Gulf of Mexico, deploying as far west as Hawaii when required, since its peacetime

VOLANT EYE operations cover the eastern Pacific as well as the Caribbean, Gulf of Mexico, and Atlantic Ocean. Refinements of that basic task, which are continuing requirements, include VOLANT COAST (winter recco of the Atlantic coast and the Gulf), VOLANT MET (weather recco in areas of sparse data such as the Gulf of Alaska) for the USAF Global Weather Center, and VOLANT CROSS, when the Herks of the 158th precede eastern Pacific crossing by TAC aircraft.

Carter uses overhead projections to refresh my knowledge of hurricanes.

Giant low-pressure cells that turn upon themselves for energy and build to destructive forces, counterclockwise rotation, winds increasing in velocity as you approach the center, a calm eye only a few miles in diameter with blue skies above and bordered by the most fierce weather of all — a circular wall of great mature thunderstorms that feature torrential rains and extreme turbulence.

I have no trouble following him so far. After all, forty years ago my white-knuckled hands gripped the yoke of an ancient PBM-5S Mariner as we made hurricane penetrations in the first tentative days of storm investigation. I can relate to the unbelievable winds and frightening turbulence.

The aircraft make investigative flights into developing storms at 1,500 feet to see if hurricane potential is there. Penetration of a full-blown

hurricane is made at 10,000 feet, usually on cardinal headings. The purpose of the flights is to locate the center of the storm and determine its course and speed. We do horizontal and vertical weather reporting.

Colonel Gates adds a pilot's perspective.

We penetrate with the wind off our left wing. That insures we are always flying directly toward the eye. Airspeed is 180 knots. We follow the navigator's directions exactly, as it is his responsibility to keep track of the wind direction and we must keep our heading perpendicular to it, especially as we near the wall that surrounds the eye. Hit that at the wrong angle and the storm will literally spit you right back into the intense clouds and you have a real exciting time.

That brings to mind a question. I know that even the mighty Hercules can be overextended in a violent storm, and a hurricane certainly falls into that category. How do you know when you should abort and try another day?

Gates grins.

It's a judgement call . . . based on experience. If you do it right — the penetration, that is — you can handle it, but there are times, such as the loss of your radar, when you turn around and take the safest way back out. You have to have all of your equipment working.

I'd ride with Gates into one. He has more than a decade of such experience and some telltale gray hair. Pilots with gray hair impress me. I know how they got them and while each strand may reveal a moment of terror, it also reveals a good decision.

The rest of the briefing is routine, including the crew briefing. I'm scheduled to fly a short weather flight and I meet my hosts.

"Hi, I'm Major Wheeler. This is my copilot,

Framed in a sister Herk's open cargo doors, a weather WC-130 enjoys a rare moment of calm flight.

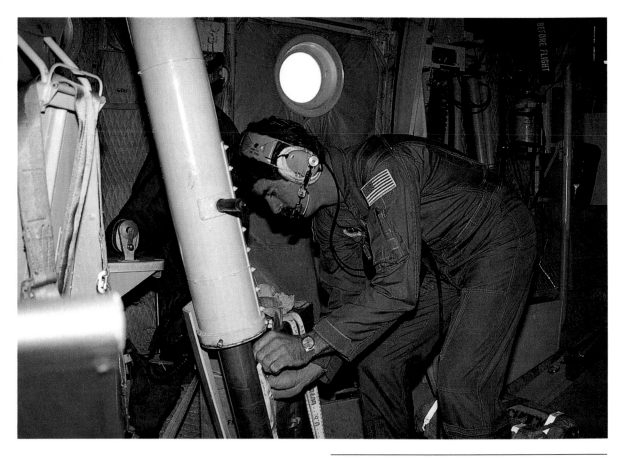

Major Bourgueois; navigator, Lieutenant Colonel Tures; Major McIntosh, our ARWO [aerial reconnaissance weather officer]; our extra pilot, Major Little; flight engineer Senior Master Sergeant Davis; and weather observer/dropsonde operator, Master Sergeant Robert E. Lee.''

It seems like I've heard the dropsonde operator's name before.

In the aircraft (WC-130H, call sign 037) I am assigned the right-hand weather observer's seat, a position in the forward section of the cargo bay opposite a large viewing window. At 0930, we lift from the Keesler runway and turn out to sea.

The main hurricane month for the Gulf is September, although the season extends from June 1 through November 30; nevertheless, at the

60

weather briefing I felt quite reassured. There simply is no weather of consequence within our patrol area this day. Blue skies.

I visit the flight deck and chat with the crew, noting the station of the ARWO. Before long we are ready to make our first dropsonde drop. I return back aft to observe Robert E. Lee. As I do so, I glance at the sturdy structure of the aircraft. A hurricane rider must have, above all, strength and reliability. Smashing through that eye wall is not for the fainthearted — man or machine — and the turbulence can shake the strongest airplane with the forces of Hades itself. Wings flex, and anything not tied down or secured can be turned into dangerous, even lethal, projectiles. Engines surge as rapid g changes affect fuel flow and delicate computer-controlled system components. Instrument panels vibrate with unbelievable fury — you try your darnedest to

Sergeant Lee reads and relays dropsonde data back to a central collection point for inclusion in the national weather forecast.

see the instruments but they become blurs. A torrent of heavy rain slams against the windscreen and pounds on the metal surfaces of the aircraft with the sound of a thousand banshees trying to penetrate the aluminum with ball-peen hammers. Lightning is frequently encountered. It isn't a bad idea to keep the cockpit lights up at low-visibility times of the day; you avoid temporary flash blindness that way. And where there is lightning there is thunder, and while you may not hear it the forces that create it slam against your already battered aircraft. You are thrown against your seats, and your seat belt and shoulder harness cut into your body as your hands and feet constantly work the yoke and rudders to prevent the aircraft from being tossed into an out-of-control attitude. That's the ultimate danger, for such a situation adds additional stress to that already imposed by the storm. Structural limits can be exceeded, even during the recovery.

The ride into the hurricane starts off rough, gets rougher as you penetrate, becomes downright violent as you hit the wall, and then becomes unbelievably smooth as you enter the eye and circle within the calm of the storm. Your sense of relief is marred by only one thought: You have to do it all over again to get back out.

But the Hercules wing is thick and sinewy, with special aluminum alloy construction, and those four Allisons are as reliable as any engine

Cruising on top, a WC-130 makes final preparations for a wild ride into the storm to determine direction and strength. All loose items are secured and the crew firmly strapped in.

ever built. The C-130 has positive stability around all three axes and a responsive control system. With a skilled crew, hurricane penetration can be a relatively safe, albeit very uncomfortable, occurrence.

Such thoughts are academic today, however, as 037 rides the calm air in a cloudless sky. Robert E. Lee ("call me Bob") is getting ready to do his thing. He completes loading the dropsonde (a three-pound cylindrical device, 18.5 inches long and 3.5 inches in diameter) into its launching tube just as I arrive, and he gives me a few brief moments of explanation while he waits for the drop signal from the weather officer. Master Sergeant Lee is a professional and he is eager to explain his job to me. In his position as dropsonde operator, he also takes on crew duties that would normally be assigned to a loadmaster.

The Omega dropwindsonde system (ODWS) consists of a launching tube, expendable dropsondes, and an on-board computer that receives the dropsonde radio signals by keyboard entry. A pair of teleprinters record real time data (there are some variations in equipment).

Today we drop at 18,000 feet (the sondes are effective at any height below 40,000 feet) and the dropsonde will transmit pressure, temperature, humidity, and contribute to wind data determination every ten seconds (roughly every 167 feet of fall) until it hits the surface.

Sergeant Lee returns to his console and begins receiving and editing the radiosonde's coded signals, insuring that they are accurate before transmitting the formatted data by voice to a central collection agency. Hurricane data goes directly from the aircraft to the National Hurricane Center in Miami, a Department of Commerce activity.

Today, there is little to report except for an isothermal layer down around 10,000 feet.

In this day of weather satellites it is natural to wonder why the necessity for aircraft investigation of hurricanes and major storms. I remember Gates's answer to that question when I asked it at the preflight briefing.

The satellite shows us the storm, and roughly where it is, and over a period of time its movement. But the National Hurricane Center needs more than that to provide an accurate forecast of its strength and its probable direction. Only data from the penetrating aircraft can provide the wind velocity in the various quadrants and the temperature and pressure gradients, which are a clue to the intensity of the storm. Sometimes the eye is obscured by upper-level clouds and we can't pinpoint it by satellite . . . it takes penetration.

Herk, you old rascal, even high-technology satellites can't steal your thunder.

Take heart! Help is on the way in the form of a 129th ARRS (Aerospace Rescue and Recovery Squadron) HC-130P and accompanying Blackhawks.

Chapter 6
The Seagoing Herks

The United States Navy received its first Hercules in July 1960: four LC-130Fs, B-model ski conversions, BuNos 148318, 148319, 148320, and 148321. The skibirds immediately became the mainstay of the Navy's special mission antarctic squadron. The USMC had been operating several KC-130F tankers since their first delivery to the Corps back in March of the same year, and the Coast Guard had been flying the HC-130B since December 1959. Later on, the Navy was to acquire the DC-130A drone carrier for VC (Composite) squadrons; the EC-130Q for its VQ (long-range communications platforms) squadrons; the C-130F/G for VR (fleet logistic support) use; and the LC-130R, H-model ski conversion, to augment their south polar squadron, VXE-6. Since 1969 a solitary USMC KC-130 has been assigned to the Navy's flight demonstration squadron, the Blue Angels.

Military airlift, of course, is the responsibility of MAC, so the Navy has never operated a substantial C-130 fleet, confining its Hercules requirements to marine corps tankers, antarctic scientific research support, tactical fleet communications, drone operations, and logistic fleet support. The VR Herks range worldwide, delivering high-priority cargo and passengers to fleet support activities. As of 1987, the Navy and Marine Corps had received 111 Herks, a very small number of which have been lost to normal operations.

When we think of Naval Air, we naturally think of carrier operations, and the amazing Hercules became the largest, heaviest, and most-engined aircraft ever to operate from an aircraft carrier. With the advent of the larger bird farms, particularly the nukes, aerial logistic supply of task forces at sea became an expanding requirement. The COD (carrier onboard delivery) aircraft of the early 60s were the Grumman C-1 Trader, a logistic modification of the tried and true S2 antisubmarine airplane, and the newly emerging slightly larger and more capable Grumman C-2A Greyhound. Twin-engined, with only modest range and limited personnel and cargo capacity, the C-1 was hard-pressed to meet fleet requirements. While the C-2A sported fuel-efficient turboprop engines (thus better speed, altitude, and range) and a rear cargo loading door, why not look at an even larger, more capable

---

The skied LC-130Rs of the National Science Foundation's antarctic research effort are crewed and maintained by personnel of VXE-6, the U.S. Navy's special mission volunteer squadron. The giant skis (world's largest) are Teflon-coated to reduce takeoff and landing friction.

A USMC KC-130T tanker refuels a pair of Sikorsky CH-53D Sea Stallions that in turn have LAVs (light armored vehicles) slung below them.

transport/cargo type?

Why not a Hercules C-130?

Carrier Ops

October 30, 1963. The USS *Forrestal* (CVA-59) plowed through the ever-moving Atlantic off our East coast. A slight ground swell eased the big carrier up and down gently as it steamed along, a light chop slapping against its bow. From time to time a conflicting secondary swell system was encountered; the bow of the *Forrestal* would rise and fall and the great ship would develop a slight but certainly perceptible roll. A special dotted white centerline was painted along the axial deck from the forward lip aft to the recovery edge of the flight deck. Normal flight operations were about to begin. Normal? Well, almost normal, at least for ship's company. Jerry Daugherty, a seasoned LSO (landing signal officer), manned his station as the *Forrestal* turned to bring forty knots of relative wind down the flight deck. PriFly (primary flight control, the ship's equivalent of an airport control tower) reported all in readiness and the captain of the *Forrestal* gave the order, "Recover Aircraft."

Downwind, Hercules BuNo 149798, a KC-130F on loan from the Marine Corps, steadied itself, and the pilot, Lt. James H. Flatley, U.S. Navy, directed that the landing gear be lowered. As the twin-tandem main gear and dual nose gear snapped into their locked position, Flatley and his copilot, Lt. Comdr. W. W. Stovall, with the assistance of their flight engineer, Aviation Mechanic First Class E. F. Brennan, completed their downwind landing checks. Observing their procedures was the only other occupant of the flight deck, Ted H. Limmer, Jr., a Lockheed engineering test pilot. The Hercules rolled left onto its base leg. The marine C-130, with a navy crew, was about to enter the history books.

It all started back on October 8 when 9798 was delivered to the Naval Air Test Center in Patuxent River, Maryland. A Forrestal-class deck was outlined on one of the runways, and Flatley and his crew had flown several weeks of simulated carrier landings at weights from 80,000 pounds up to 100,000 pounds. The large refueling pods, normal equipment of tanker Herks, had been removed, a slight reduction in the nose gear aperture had been made, and a Hytrol antiskid braking system Mark 3 (used on the Boeing 727 commercial transport) had been substituted for the Hercules' normal system. One of the objectives of the field carrier work, in addition to mastering the low-speed flying characteristics of the C-130 and nailing down the pattern altitudes and airspeeds, was to achieve a sink rate of not more than 9 fps (feet per second). Flatley was pleasantly surprised to find that he could do even better than that — 5.6 fps. That factor alone would be a critical consideration when the heavy Herk was brought to the CUT position and settled onto the deck of the *Forrestal*. Flatley rapidly developed the necessary feel of the Hercules; after all, he was a very experienced carrier aviator and enjoyed an outstanding professional reputation among his peers. (Nevertheless, his reported first words upon hearing he was being assigned to bring the C-130 on board a carrier were, "You've got to be kidding!")

Flatley and his crew concentrated on the relatively tiny CVA landing platform as they continued their turn through base and onto final. They had a comforting number of landings and takeoffs back at Patuxent under their belts, but the landing platform slowly sliding into position off their nose was not a static concrete runway. It was moving. Up, down, and from side to side. The movements were not extreme, just about par for normal carrier operations, but those operations required the ultimate in precision control of an aircraft. Flatley already had a number of approaches to the *Forrestal* under his belt, setting up his pattern and checking the feel of the Hercules on final. This time, however, he would land.

Rock steady, he drove the Hercules down the landing path, received a hearty CUT from Daugherty, and let the Hercules continue on to touchdown. As the aircraft plopped solidly onto the flight deck, aligned perfectly with the centerline, Flatley added full power. The C-130 roared past

the "island" with only fifteen feet of wing-tip clearance and lifted back into the air. The onlooking ship's crew cheered and chuckled as they read the inscription "Look ma, no hook!" boldly painted on the right side of the C-130.

Flatley and his aircrew made twenty-nine touch-and-goes and twenty-one full-stop landings and takeoffs that day (the actual number varies with several accounts), lifting off into the forty-knot headwind at airspeeds varying between sixty and eighty knots. The weight of the Hercules varied from 121,000 pounds to 92,000 pounds as fuel was consumed. On his full-stop landings, Flatley actually placed his engine condition levers into their full reverse detents before the gear contacted the flight deck!

On November 21 and 22, Flatley and his crew repeated their outstanding performance, shooting seven touch-and-goes and seventeen full stops, including seventeen takeoffs from the angled deck at weights of 90,000 pounds!

The Navy had demonstrated that COD delivery by Hercules was possible with resupply ranges of 2,500 miles and a cargo capacity of 25,000 pounds within its capability, but there were overriding considerations. One, the Hercules was just a bit too large; there would be insufficient maneuvering room on the flight deck with an air group embarked despite the C-130's ability to back down. Two, if the C-130 experienced a grounding discrepancy, where did you put it? It was too large for the elevator and hangar deck and topside stowage would seriously jeopardize, if not preclude, normal flight operations. Modifying the Herk's wings and tail assembly for folding was not considered feasible. And finally, the C-2A Greyhound was developing nicely.

So the navy community of Herk drivers was

denied its moment in the sun as carrier pilots (not too many moans were heard) and Flatley was awarded the Distinguished Flying Cross for his airmanship skill and crew leadership. Later on he became a rear admiral. He along with Stovall, Brennan, and Limmer remain the only carrier-qualified Hercules crew.

Look ma, no hook! The world's largest and heaviest carrier-qualified aircraft shoots a touch-and-go aboard the USS *Forrestal* (CVA-59). The program was later dropped—but what a thought!

TACAMO

What does a Hercules providing long-range stra-tegic communications relay between our National Command Center and submerged on-station nuclear submarines have in common with a flying missionary delivering critical medical supplies by air to a remote jungle tribe living in the vast rain forests of Brazil?

Tactics.

Tactics?

Yes. The flying missionary, in order to lower medical supplies onto a small clearing in the jungle, will set his Cessna into a steep bank and lower the supplies on the end of a rope. The physics of the rope dangling from a tightly circling aircraft cause it to become practically vertical with its end "stationary" and it can be held over the clearing.

A navy C-130Q can perform a similar maneuver, a constant thirty-degree bank for example, and dangle its long trailing wire antenna out a special opening in its cargo ramp until the wire is almost vertical. We all know that a very low-frequency antenna radiates most efficiently in a vertical position, right? And we are talking *long* vertical antenna in this case — two to five miles.

The Navy's TACAMO (take charge and move out is one explanation of the acronym) VQ squadrons are responsible for communications relay to strategic naval forces. Considered survivable even in the event of a widespread nuclear war, aircraft from squadrons at Patuxent and Guam provide these services and are barely distinguishable from the transport Herks, only small wingtip pods and a few unique antennae betraying their vital mission. Since the inception of the TACAMO squadrons, the Hercules assigned have been updated with more modern avionics through the TACAMO II, III, and IV programs. While the IV mods aren't discussed in mixed company (us and them), the previous mods have resulted in reduced weight of the communications package and a tie-in with the U.S. Worldwide Command and Control System (WWCCS), which insures survivability of communications between the National Command Authority, SAC, and submerged submarines. Soon to be replaced by more capable aircraft, the low-profile C-130Qs carry out their vital missions around the clock, unsung and unnoticed. They prefer it that way.

Marine Herks

The carrier-qualified Hercules on loan from the Marine Corps is only one of a small fleet of tactical KC-130Fs (and some T and R models) that the USMC flies in support of its air support VMF (fighter) and VMA (attack) squadrons. A vital part of the air-ground team that is a marked characteristic of the Marine Corps, the aerial tankers of the three active-duty MAWs (marine air wings) operate under the control of Marine Aerial Refueling Transport Squadrons VMGR-152, VMGR-252, VMGR-253, and VMGR-352. A fourth group, VMGR-234 of the Reserve MAW-4, also provides valuable support, its training and operational flights being incorporated into the support of active-duty forces.

The Blue Angels' USMC-operated KC-130T, "Fat Albert," gets into the act with a stunning rocket-assisted takeoff. Hornet drivers, pfffft!

Lt. Kay Griffiths-Rossi is representative of the new generation of antarctic Hercules pilots—young, highly skilled, and intensely motivated.

Indicative of the tactical importance of USMC Hercules tankers is their impressive record of refueling marine fighters and attack aircraft on over-water deployment flights. VMRG-352 alone provided services to sixty-one transpacific deployments between 1966 and 1970 using four tankers based at Futema, Okinawa, with the balance of their aircraft on the West Coast. Among the refueled aircraft were F-4s, F-8s, A-6s, A-3s, and A-4s, and not a single one was lost.

As for their tanker versatility, USMC KC-130Fs and Ts have been cleared for service to A-4, A-6, A-7, F-4, F-5, F-8, F-9, F-11, F-14, F-18, F-101, F-105, AV-8, and OV-1 fixed-wing aircraft and HH-3E and CH-53E helicopters!

The KC-130 tankers use the reeled hose, drogue basket system and are capable of refueling two aircraft simultaneously.

Marine corps representation in the Navy's Blue Angel Squadron consists of a marine crew and a USMC KC-130F tanker, BuNo 149806. The Herk, dubbed Fat Albert, wears the brightly painted blue and gold color scheme of squadron aircraft and provides transportation and logistic support for the heavily committed navy flight demonstration squadron, overseas as well as in-country. Occasionally, Fat Albert demonstrates a spectacular rocket-assisted takeoff (RATO), firing eight solid rocket bottles simultaneously, four on each side of the fuselage just ahead of the paratrooper exit doors. The maximum performance leap invariably elicits oohs and ahhs as well as a spontaneous ovation from excited onlookers.

Antarctic Operations

The Navy also operates the largest ski-equipped aircraft in the world, the LC-130R (and a pair of the older LC-130F models). The massive main skis are twenty feet long and five and a half feet wide, the nose ski is ten feet long and equally wide, and the entire assembly weighs 4,200 pounds. The bottoms of all three skis are coated with Teflon to reduce surface friction when sliding across the snow and ice, and their retracted position with the gear down allows normal landings on hard-surface runways.

Antarctic Development Squadron Six (VXE-6) is unique among navy units: it has no fleet operating or fleet support mission within its primary purpose. (However, the author vividly remembers being pressed into combat service during the 1965 Dominican Republic political crisis. Imagine a ski-equipped C-130 delivering combat-ready marines at the semitropical San Ysidro airport.) The squadron exists primarily to support U.S. scientific research efforts in Antarctica. The current-day squadron is an outgrowth of an all-volunteer unit that began extensive antarctic flying back in 1956. The early C-47s, P2Vs, and C-54s of the antarctic squadron were soon operated to their limits, and as antarctic exploration and research expanded it became obvious that a more capable aircraft was needed. The USAF had been operating ski-Herks in the arctic for some time and brought several down to Antarctica to demonstrate their capability. Their performance was impressive and the Navy ordered four aircraft, which were delivered in 1960 and deployed for the DEEPFREEZE 61 season (September 1960 to February 1961).

Since that time, the ski-Herks have proven to be invaluable, opening up the entire continent to air access and pioneering air routes from South America, Australia, and Africa to Antarctica.

Today, VXE-6 operates five LC-130Rs and two LC-130Fs, the aircraft actually being owned by the National Science Foundation. An additional LC-130F has been reclaimed after a sixteen-year storage under antarctic snows! This Herk, one of the original four assigned, suffered a takeoff accident at a field camp, Dome Charlie, during DEEPFREEZE 72. In the ensuing years all but three feet of the vertical tail were covered by the constantly blowing antarctic snows. During the 1986–87 season, personnel under the guidance of Lockheed technical representatives dug out the buried Hercules and pulled it up a snow incline to the surface. During the 1987–88 season, new engines were hung and the aircraft was flown back to McMurdo for eventual return to New Zealand for overhaul. The remarkable

A snow landing is like any other landing, once you get by the hidden crevasses and rough sastrugi (ice ridges).

recovery operation is typical of the astounding field repair and maintenance that squadron personnel have achieved with the guidance and assistance of Lockheed tech reps. Themselves experts in C-130 construction and systems, the tech reps have provided superb guidance in such extensive salvage operations as complete wing changes in the field! And we're talking frigid antarctic outdoors high on the antarctic ice sheet 700 miles from McMurdo. The hearty Lockheed specialists have worked side by side with navy personnel since the introduction of the Hercules to antarctic operations, as have Allison engine representatives who have also been a vital part of the civilian support team.

The Hercules operations are augmented by extensive navy helicopter usage, VXE-6 utilizing the Bell UH-1N Hueys as strenuously as they employ their Herks.

Crewmen of the Navy's VXE-6 squadron maintain their aircraft in the frigid open air of Antarctica. Even engines are changed in the great outdoors.

It has been more than twenty-one years since I set foot in VXE-6 spaces, but as I approach their hangar at the Pacific Missile Test Center in Point Mugu, California, all of the old memories flood back. Outside on the ramp sit four LC-130Rs and old 319, one of the first LC-130Fs. I've done time in 319. I climb the steps to the second-level office spaces and am ushered into the skipper's office.

Commander Jack B. Rector, U.S. Navy, is the latest in a thirty-one-year-long succession of VXE-6 squadron commanders. He welcomes me warmly and offers me the traditional navy coffee.

Rector has followed the time-proven succession to command — a year as ops boss, a year as XO, and now an experienced Hercules pilot and well-seasoned commanding officer. Seated opposite me, he leans forward as we discuss squadron operations then and now. Much is the same, some is better, some has been lost. His main concern is the National Science Foundation's (NSF) rumblings about making antarctic Herk operations a year-round program.

We can do it, but NSF has to be prepared to realize what it will cost. . . . Hell, I'd need a squadron almost twice this size and they will have to be prepared for the inevitable delays and downed aircraft in the winter darkness.

Prior to their regular five-month deployment (October through February), VXE-6 annually flies to the white continent during the late winter months — their WINFLY operation — but makes only one or two flights from Christchurch in August to meet early scientific requirements. And successful flights have been flown in the middle of the winter darkness; I am a veteran of one, myself.

Our airplanes go into overhaul every off-season due to the hard battering they take in the months on the Ice. I usually have only one for training, and with a three-year turnover, we have to conduct summer training. We have no search and rescue backup for austral winter antarctic operations and that is a must.

That requirement has already received attention. Several brand-new skied Air National Guard Hercules (New York) are being considered for duty as SAR aircraft during off-season fly-ins. We discuss the issue for over an hour, both agreeing that such a step must be carefully considered and safety must be a paramount consideration. A succession of successful WINFLYs over the past years is not the same as extensive winter operations. WINFLYs are carefully scheduled and meticulously planned, with good weather forecasts a must, along with a four-hour daylight window. They are flexible, one or two day's adjustment being no problem. A regular schedule, in darkness and all types of antarctic weather (and winter is the fiercest), is quite another ball game.

So, along with his long days of preparation and planning for deployment (only a few days away as we talk), an anticipation of around-the-clock duty for the next five months, and a genuine concern for the safety of his people and the well-being of the families left behind, Rector must find time to look ahead and formulate his input to expanded requirements by NSF.

There is a light knock on his door. At his acknowledgment, two young lieutenants walk in. Rector has offered to let me discuss current operations with two of his people. He makes the introductions.

Lieutenant Kay Griffiths-Rossi, one of our Hercules pilots . . . and this is Lieutenant Cheryl Erickson. Cheryl just reported aboard and along with Lieutenant Griffiths-Rossi just returned from our WINFLY operation.

I note the gold navigator's wings on Erickson's jacket patch. Good. A pilot and navigator, both veterans of an off-season flight. We leave Commander Rector to his busy schedule and the two officers escort me out to one of the LC-130Rs. We climb up onto the flight deck and I take a moment to look around. Very little difference from the F model, notably the navigator's station with the INS and updated panel.

Lieutenant Griffiths-Rossi, who is married to one of the squadron helo pilots, leans casually against the back of the pilot's seat, grinning broadly as we start to talk about the Herk.

I like it. Nice airplane. It's versatile . . . it doesn't go fast, doesn't look beautiful, but it holds a lot and will go almost anyplace you want it to go.

I ask them about the August WINFLY operation.

Both officers laugh and shake their heads in the time-honored manner of aviators who can see humor in the most serious of things — afterward.

Cheryl and I were both on one crew. We arrived at McMurdo early due to unexpected tailwinds and it was still dark. We had number two feathered due to a suspected fuel leak . . . milled around and finally decided to try a night pass. The landing lights worked well and lit up the surface, so we landed, along with our second aircraft. The snow was really soft. We had to shut down both port engines so the maintenance people could look for the fuel leak. We didn't find anything wrong and there was no evidence of a leak. During the restart we found out the number two engine starter was frozen . . . that caused some concern as we didn't want to spend the rest of the winter at McMurdo! On top of it all the weather was turning sour. . . . On the soft snow we could only get forty-five knots so we made runs to pack the snow and made it off okay, right after the other aircraft. That was the first time I've actually had problems on take-off. Most of the flying is off prepared surfaces . . . I only had one open field last season.

Cheryl chimes in with her observation of the event.

That was an eventful day for you because you had to shut down an engine twenty minutes out, then a night landing on an unprepared surface . . . on skis . . . and then we had all those problems getting off . . . a long day. Well over

twenty-four hours.

Griffiths-Rossi is a product of the Aviation Officers' Candidate program. After receiving her wings at Pensacola she went through multiengine training (Beechcraft T-44s at Corpus Christi) and then attended the USAF C-130 training course at Little Rock Air Force Base. Erickson, a product of the NROTC program at the University of Rochester, is a seasoned navigator, having reported to VXE-6 from a VP (Patrol) squadron just prior to the WINFLY. She recalls the difference in navigation requirements.

In P-3s I was basically a systems operator . . . the little black boxes did all the work. I get here and find I have to go back to basics and learn navigating all over again. We can't use our INS on the Ice as the hard landings and takeoffs wreak havoc with the gear's gyros and accelerometers, so we use sun lines and radar and dead reckoning.

Griffiths-Rossi laughs and slings a gentle needle at Erickson. *You just can't love an INS like you can love a sextant.*

I inquire as to the use of grid navigation, the polar system of artificial latitude lines that place the south pole at a navigational equator.

Yes . . . we still have to use it due to not being able to rely on our INS, and because of the large magnetic variations in the polar region.

Kay Griffiths-Rossi jumps in with an example. I gather it is about a crew with pilots named Lewis and Clark, a not-too-unfamiliar pair of names. *On the Lewis and Clark expedition to Byrd Station, the crew relied on the INS system for their return flight to McMurdo. After a while they noticed they were over water. One of them asked if they were supposed to be. That was the first recognition that something was wrong with the INS. They wandered around a bit before coming back to McMurdo.* The Lewis and Clark expedition obviously is now part of the squadron's folklore.

Erickson continues talking about her navigation duties:

The INS is used mostly just to give ground speed and drift angle. You can compute winds and DR [dead reckon] from it so there's some confidence factor. As for Loran, we remove the Loran from the aircraft before we go to the Ice . . . there's no Loran coverage in Antarctica.

Griffiths-Rossi takes over again.

As for the radio altimeter — the green worm as we affectionately know it — it is primarily for our transpac flight since you must use it over water and not too much over any kind of snow terrain. We fly an augmented crew on the Ice: three pilots, one or two navigators, two flight engineers, two loadmasters or one loadmaster plus a utility crewman, primarily because of the long days of eighteen hours or so. There's lots of time flight planning and frequent delays at en route stops due to cargo requirements and weather changes.

As the two women talk, I think of the contrast with the antarctic pilots of my day. Usually senior high-time aviators and often heavily bearded, the Herk drivers of the 60s have been superseded by the modern professionals of today's Navy — and these two need take a backseat to none of their predecessors. Knowledgeable about the aircraft and its systems, enthusiastic about their flying opportunities, and confident of their skills, they can fly and talk Herk with the best of their peers. Griffiths-Rossi is a T2P (transport second

pilot) and is looking forward to qualifying as a PTAC (polar transport aircraft commander) on the approaching deployment. As such, she will join an elite community of Hercules drivers who have landed their aircraft on unseen surfaces during whiteout conditions, conducted internally guided radar approaches down to zero-zero minimums, and exercised their own weather forecasting while flying over a continent half again as big as the United States but with only fifteen to twenty reporting weather stations (there are more than that in Colorado alone). Her crewmate, Cheryl Erickson, will join an equally elite group of polar navigators who retain the basic skills of dead reckoning and celestial and sun navigation as well as operators of the more sophisticated INS and Omega navigation systems. The antarctic pilot and navigator are their own breed and fly without the frills of sophisticated air traffic control. Among all those who fly, they alone must still combine the techniques of the bush pilot with the advanced skills of the 80s naval aviation community.

As we leave the flight deck — it *is* Friday afternoon and well into happy hour time, and the base is throwing a going-away bash for its antarctic squadron — I thank the two impressive young lieutenants and stop by the squadron spaces to wish Commander Rector well. I take a final glance at the Hercules line as I leave. I won't accept Griffiths-Rossi and Erickson's invitation to join the squadron at the O club happy hour. It's their squadron now, not mine.

A few months later, I learn of the loss of one of the LC-130Rs on the Ice. Two fatalities, the first VXE-6 Hercules deaths in DEEP-FREEZE. It is like a death in my family.

Chapter 7
Semper Paratus Herks

Back in 1790, when Secretary of the Treasury Alexander Hamilton commissioned a small fleet of ten "revenue cutters" to enforce the revenue laws of the United States, he could hardly have foreseen the scope of the twentieth century mission of the young nation's coastal guard forces. The smallest of our armed services (1987 personnel strength: 38,000), the United States Coast Guard has assumed responsibilities far beyond its apparent limitation of size. Noted for its dedication, effectiveness, efficiency, and preparedness, the service has a tenacious will to fight when called upon to do so. Veterans of the War of 1812 and the Civil War as well as every other conflict that has tasked the United States, the Coasties have proven themselves true guardians of our nation, and when called upon, extremely valuable adjuncts to our Navy.

Today, with an annual budget of less than two billion dollars the Coast Guard not only fulfills its traditional roles of enforcing our tariff laws and providing among other things surveillance and assistance to boats and ships in coastal

waters and high seas, it has taken on the demanding tasks of offshore law enforcement (LE missions) and the enforcement of a multitude of laws and treaties (ELT missions). Every one of the 38,000 Coast Guard men and women — who altogether would be lost in the home stadium of the Denver Broncos — is critical to the USCG purpose, and they man 250 cutters, 2,000 smaller boats, and a significant air force while operating out of more than 1,500 shore units, most with less than 50 people assigned. Among their more mundane tasks have been the checking and maintaining of both the Loran and Omega worldwide navigational systems.

The Coast Guard has the primary responsibility for the defense of our coastlines within an integrated coast guard/navy plan involving a number of maritime defense zones around the United States. And while the military threat to our coastlines is of no great concern at the moment, there is a devastating assault by the hordes of illegal aliens who make their way from Caribbean island homes toward the United States. Notable have been the Haitian boat people. Add to those unfortunates the even greater threat of illegal drug running and you realize that the Gulf of Mexico and the Caribbean Sea form a vast no-man's-

---

A pond of snow melt gives a surrealistic reflection to a Kodiak-based USCG Hercules.

land between the drug capitals of South and Central America and the lucrative U.S. market. There is a very real maritime war going on and smack in the middle of it is the United States Coast Guard. And one of our most valuable assets in that war are the Coastie Herks.

The brilliantly painted white Hercules, with highly visible orange and blue stripes wrapped around their forward fuselages and another swath of orange on their vertical tails, operate from six Coast Guard air stations: Kodiak, Alaska; Barbers Point, Hawaii; McClellan Air Force Base, California; Elizabeth City, North Carolina; Clearwater, Florida; and Borinquen, Puerto Rico (formerly Ramey Air Force Base). Predominantly HC-130Hs, the Hercules actually roam the world carrying out their USCG tasks, but each air station has prime responsibilities. From Kodiak, it is the arctic waters and close surveillance of fishing activities; from Coast Guard Air Station Kodiak fly seven USCG Hercules. Four Herks provide Hawaiian and Pacific waters coverage from Barbers Point. From McClellan, four Hercules patrol the north Pacific and conduct similar fishing law surveillance. Elizabeth City is the home of the USCG Aviation Maintenance and Supply Depot as well as much of the Coast Guard's air training activities. The air station's operational responsibilities start with the Atlantic coastline and include arctic ice patrols flown out of Newfoundland; four to five Hercules fly from there. The Clearwater Air Station, which has the most demanding tasks of all, operates in concert with Borinquen; on top of routine lifesaving, shipping assistance, and maritime surveillance, Clearwater has the frontline responsibilities in the Caribbean and Gulf drug wars. The H-model Hercules that comprise the long-range patrol and interdiction force are configured especially for that role.

The long-range and low-speed controllability of the Hercules make it particularly adaptable for the tactics of maritime patrol and shipping surveillance. Able to proceed to on-station at high fuel-conserving altitudes, the Hercules drops and leisurely cruises at its 1,000–5,000-foot visual and radar search altitude. Its INS insures that a predetermined search pattern is closely followed. The aircraft is equipped with a full set of communication gear (the entire crew enjoys full communication capability) from VHF and UHF through the HF spectrum normally employed by ships at sea. Its avionics package also includes wide-ranging DF (direction finding) gear. Secure voice is available for classified traffic, as is a series of coded geographical points that can be used to give plain-language bearing-and-distance locations of surface traffic. The Coastie Hercules carry their normal complement of lifesaving and maritime assistance gear, from life jackets and rafts to survival supplies and droppable bilge pumps. Built into the lower cargo ramp is a series of ten flare tubes, remotely controlled from either of the two forward scanner positions. (Some minor differences in configuration are present in the HC-130H series; some earlier aircraft have large observation windows in the two aft paratrooper doors, for example.) The scanners, one on each side of the forward fuselage, have large, square viewing windows and a small padded shelf to support them when leaning forward. The entire crew sits strapped in special sheepskin-covered seats that are almost fully reclinable and have multiadjustments including both lumbar and thigh support. A ten- or twelve-hour patrol can induce considerable fatigue, and efficiency can drop. The seats fight that tendency, providing a relaxing and changeable support for each crew member.

On the flight deck, the pilots can employ an autopilot that is flexible enough to provide for low-altitude, slow-speed maneuvering and is coupled to the INS for track following; it can also be coupled with the Omega navigation system. To aid visual search and identification, a pair of gyro-stabilized field glasses are available. There are no crew rest bunks, the space taken up by the radioman's position. (Some special maritime patrol aircraft [HC-130MP] feature an optional roll-in roll-out crew rest module, which contains bunks and a galley.)

With the USCG C-130Bs (no external fuel tanks), an early low-altitude search tactic was to secure the two outboard engines and cruise on the inboards, thereby effecting some extension of time on station. However, current patrols (or searches) in the longer-ranged H-model Hercules normally utilize all four engines for greater patrol speed and greater safety in low-altitude maneuvering. Patrol duration can normally be kept below twelve hours and the fuel supply is ample for a four-engine operation.

Working in concert with the U.S. Customs Office, the USCG Hercules scour the routes used by drug traffickers, concentrating their search on the natural "choke-point" waterways between Cuba and the Yucatan Peninsula, between Cuba and Haiti, and between the many island groups of the West Indies. Surface traffic down to the smallest seagoing vessels is visually identified by low-altitude flybys, and the characteristics and names of vessels encountered are radioed to central collection and monitoring stations. Suspicious craft are tracked and turned over to USCG, U.S. Navy, or U.S. Customs surface

A USCG loadmaster prepares to drop a survival package should it be required by an endangered surface vessel.

intercepters as the situation develops. Coast Guard cutters carry the Aerospatiale HH-65 helicopters, which are employed when within range of contacts. USCG rotary-winged aircraft, Sikorsky HH-3s, also work with Bahamian boarding parties in a multinational effort to intercept the drug boats.

In the fore of this effort is Coast Guard Air Station Clearwater in Florida. Positioned on the east side of the Clearwater/St. Petersburg International Airport, the air station is home for fifty officers and three hundred enlisted personnel. Housed in two cantilevered rectangular hangars, the station is a self-maintaining unit, providing for its own maintenance and public works support. The hangars contain shop space; stuck on

What is white and orange and seen all over? A Clearwater, Florida, Coastie Herk, with its many missions of rescue, shipping surveillance, drug patrols, prisoner lifts, and whatever.

the side of the nearest one as you drive aboard the station is an addition that houses administrative offices. On the far side of the hangar are the operations spaces, the duty office, and the flight and mission planning facilities. Most of the shops are located in the adjacent hangar. There are also a small BX, dining and living facilities, and a recreational club. Typical of USCG air stations, the grounds are neatly maintained.

There are two ready ramp pads, providing around-the-clock readiness for helicopter and Hercules duty aircraft. Inside the hangars are the off-duty helicopters and Hercules, all in various stages of repair, upkeep, or readiness. Clearwater is a quiet-appearing station and obviously among the preferred duty stations for the men and women who fly, located as it is in the popular moderate temperature belt of the central Florida coast. But appearances can be deceiving. One has only to enter those far operations spaces to realize that beyond the tranquility of the grounds there is a pace of operations that approaches, but never quite reaches, chaos. The Coasties are too professional to let little things like excessive demands upon their limited resources or daily (sometimes hourly) changes in operational requirements rattle their demeanor. After all, *semper paratus* means exactly that — always prepared. Or, at least, always flexible.

It is 0820 when I walk into the operations office. The day's flight schedule is already under attack from forces far beyond Clearwater, Florida, as government agencies faced with urgent requirements use the universal cry, "Get the Coast Guard to do it!" A dozen flight-suited men and women are busily erasing and correcting schedule boards, retyping lists, and grabbing passing aircrew members with solicitations for their availability. One concerned young lady sits at a computer keyboard, pounding away at some sort of schedule; the printer comes alive and the computer takes on a mind of its own and issues gibberish. She seems to take it all in stride, calling to no one in particular to contact the computer repair service. She recycles the print command and this time the printer sends forth an orderly flight schedule for the following day. By the time it emerges, she has several penciled changes in her hand, placed there by the phone answerers. I immediately detect that despite the activity and seemingly unorganized procedures, this is a normal day and things are getting accomplished. I have an uneasy feeling that I am intruding; these folks have plenty to do without hosting me. I am wrong, of course, for if there is one thing

the Coasties can do as well as operating, it is showing you how they do it.

"Hello . . . welcome aboard," says the friendly voice at the end of an outstretched arm. Lieutenant Commander Pat Danaher, USCG, mission planning officer for Clearwater, has timed his breathing spell for my arrival. From somewhere he produces an empty chair and offers me coffee. Sitting relaxed on his desk, his gray-green flight suit partially unzipped to provide a bit more body ventilation in the busy room, he fills me in on Clearwater's mission. Danaher is a dark-haired, picture-book naval aviator and obviously proud of his role as a coast guard officer and Herk driver. One of his first statements is that I am scheduled to go with him on a local training flight — an orientation to the area and operating procedures of the unit.

"We're due out about ten . . . local training . . . some bounce and a few GCAs over at Mac-Dill."

While he talks, I scan the master scheduling board and the pilots' training status boards. Not too many aircraft commanders but lots of blocks filled in for the up-and-coming copilots. As Danaher comments about their heavy flight requirements, I confirm them with a glance at the displayed pilot flight times. These folks get plenty of air time, that's for sure, and they get plenty of variety. I turn back my attention as he recalls a past USCG requirement to haul block ice from the Houston area to Mobile, Alabama (block ice? — "Get the Coast Guard to do it!"). A hurricane had caused severe damage to Mobile electrical power and refrigeration was a problem.

A young bear of a commander sticks his head in from an adjacent office. "Hello — you want to go on a prisoner run?"

"Or we can fly you with us to Colombia," adds another voice from across the room. "Have you got your passport with you?"

I curse myself for not thinking to bring it, but I didn't expect this kind of hospitality and assistance. As for the prisoner flight, additional discussion downgrades it on my desirability scale.

"We hauled some really bad types from Puerto Rico to the States recently. They were manacled and shackled, of course, and we had one guard per four prisoners. The governor of Puerto Rico had declared the prisons overcrowded and threatened to turn some of the inmates loose unless they were provided for elsewhere." Immediate transportation was needed to Atlanta, and Clearwater drew the assignment ("Get the Coast Guard to do it!"). They also drew the air transportation duties for some of the Cuban criminals being transferred from one federal prison facility to another.

"What a job," chimes in a young jaygee. "They couldn't be allowed to move around or get to the john so they just urinated in their pants. We hosed down the troop seats afterwards."

The opportunity clearly was not for me. Besides, those types can be dangerous and I inquired as to that possibility.

The young jaygee laughed. "On one air force C-141 flight, they raised so much hell, it took everyone except the aircraft commander to calm them down. Consequently, we preflight the aircraft and remove the fire axes and stuff they might get their hands on." Nevertheless, I positively don't want to go on a prisoner flight.

The young bear, ops boss Comdr. Kirk Colvin, laughs and allows that a drug patrol might be better for my purposes. A good man, that Colvin.

Danaher takes me on a tour of the offices and shops. As we take a break in one of the unoccupied spaces, a pert brunette sticks in her head. Another jaygee, Betty K. Uhrig, USCG. A 1984 graduate of the Coast Guard Academy at New London, Connecticut, she was a short-term exchange student at the Air Force Academy at Colorado Springs, long enough to complete the cadet gliding course there. Bitten by the flying bug, she won her wings of gold at Pensacola, graduated from the C-130 course at Little Rock Air Force Base, and has been flying Herks ever since. "A great airplane," she allows. "I like it." A rapidly progressing copilot, Uhrig is the flight records officer and eagerly describes her duties and shows me her flight record forms.

Another head appears, this time brown-haired and mustached Lt. (jg) Jeff Smith. An ex–air force helo jock, he immediately subjects himself to some good-natured ribbing by Danaher and Uhrig. Switching to the Coast Guard, he has to defend his former service, but on this day he goes down valiantly under the skilled barbs of the two Herk pilots. It seems that a number of other service aviators opt for the Coast Guard. At Clearwater, there are several ex–air force and army flyboys wearing coast guard blue and wings of gold. Subsequent conversations reveal part of the reason. There is a great deal of interesting flight time in the Coast Guard and that's the first love of any aviator-officer.

As Danaher finishes describing the drug and prisoner missions of the station, he laughs. "Funny, I joined the Coast Guard 'cause I wanted to be a fireman and I wind up a policeman!" His wide grin reveals that it's all right with him.

Later on in the day, we fly. Three hours of exhilaration in the clear blue Florida sky. Then

82

Danaher spots a sailboat and the crew makes a practice pass, with the ramp open and the load-master in position to drop a survival canister if the vessel were actually in distress. Danaher even gives me some seat time and lets me make a few turns. The Herk feels familiar — and good — even after twenty years.

Moved from St. Petersburg in 1976, Coast Guard Air Station Clearwater carries out its airborne duties with six HC-130H Hercules and six Sikorsky HH-3F Pelican helicopters. Historically, their SAR load has approximated one case per day — typically, small boaters lost or out of gas or victims of fire or storm, perhaps a general aviation crash. They yearly fly some 2,300 to 2,400 hours in such SAR work. And of course, there are the hurricanes and the accompanying disaster relief.

Crew training for the C-130 accounts for another 1,150 hours (1987 figure), a substantial increase over previous years. (The chopper training hours are also in that neighborhood — approximately 1,100 hours in 1987.)

With their obligations in the LE and ELT area ever increasing, one Hercules is pretty much committed full time, and deployments to Puerto Rico, Panama, and that U.S. garden spot of Cuba, the U.S. Naval Base at Guantánamo, are routine. Daily patrols of the Gulf and the Caribbean cover thousands of miles, and all sightings are passed to a central control as well as to applicable coast guard and navy surface vessels. Clearwater's C-130 flight hours in the drug war alone have climbed from slightly over 1,000 in 1984 to just below 4,000 in 1987. That's a chunk to lay on any small force. Once again it is a tribute to the high availability of the Hercules — and the

The long arm of the law sweeps the seas around the good old U.S. of A. Surface traffic is routinely examined, suspicious vessels tracked, and if necessary turned over to surface boarding units.

performance of the crews — that the station meets such requirements.

The contribution of the HH-3Fs should not be overlooked, since they form a valuable part of the coast guard air team, their area of responsibilities including daily patrols with Bahamian Strike Force teams on board in a multinational effort to detect and board drug boats. (Nor should we overlook the USCG HU-25A Guardian jets and their role in drug interdiction — but, hey, folks, this is a Herk book!) The choppers fly within a vulnerable envelope with respect to possible response by the bad guys, and they are being supplied with armor plate and night-vision goggles. And there is a ripple-down effect on the increase in helicopter utilization: the station

Hercules must add helo logistic support to their tasks.

With the USCG's recent acquisition of two Grumman E2C radar surveillance aircraft, the logistic demands on the Hercules have further increased. Finally there is the continuing requirement for logistic support of radar sites in the Bahamas and Caribbean.

On top of it all, the Coastie Herks find themselves assisting the Justice Department in prisoner transport, the Department of State in transporting helos to South America, and the U.S. Navy in various combined operations. (And the helo troops aid the Department of Natural Resources in red tide surveys and provide hoist training for USAF pilots.)

No wonder Air Station Clearwater claims to be the busiest operational unit in the Coast Guard and proudly displays its motto on the station insignia — Anywhere, anytime.

Drug Patrol

Eight o'clock in the morning is not really early, except on Sunday it seems like it is. As I report to the Clearwater operations duty office, the preflight activity for the day's law enforcement flight is well under way. The flight plan has been filed, the weather briefing has been received, all interested parties have been notified of the search track, and Hercules Number 1716 has been preflighted and is squatting on the hot pad, its white and orange color scheme gleaming in the warm morning sun. It's time to play the daily game of Coasties versus the Junkies, which despite the lighthearted reference is a very serious business.

Ops boss Colvin, wearing a bright international orange flight suit, will be the aircraft commander, and as we assemble in the cargo compartment for his preflight briefing I meet the other members of the crew: Lt. (jg) Chris Finnell, the copilot; Aviation Technician Steve Klindt, navigator; Aviation Metalsmith Peter Deglau, flight engineer; Aviation Technician Michael Ferreira, radioman; and scanners Terry Turner and Mike Lanning, aviation mech and machinist mate, respectively. We go over the flight route and purpose — today it's a search and rigging (identification) of boats less than 350 feet in length. Our Herk is not yet equipped with secure voice, so reports will be sent in the clear, using coded reference points. Colvin goes over the cockpit brief in detail, laying out his abort and emergency procedures and responsibilities to each of his crew members.

No questions? Box lunches on board? We're ready to go. I strap myself into a troop seat as the others man their stations. Crew chatter flows from open mikes through the intercom system, the outside observer beginning the start sequence with an "all clear" and the flight engineer responding in a monotone with instrument readings as the pilots start each of the four Allisons.

Starting number two . . . RPM . . . fuel flow . . . ignition . . . engine gear box oil pressure . . . hydraulic pressure . . . parallel . . . starter . . . series . . . temperature seven-nine-zero . . . generator on.

We taxi to runway 35, checking brakes and flaps and prop operations on the way to the run-up spot. One of the scanners walks around the cargo compartment and checks the inside hydraulic lines for leaks and peers out the small round ports in the paratrooper doors at the engines.

Dry and smooth. Everything checks out and at 0835 we lift off the runway. Colvin leans the Hercules into a gentle seaward turn as the landing gear snuggles up into its housings and the flaps slide back into their retracted position. Our assigned en route altitude is flight level 250 (25,000 feet) and we'll need the better part of an hour and a half to reach our patrol area. At 0910 we switch from Miami to Merida Control and the voice of a Mexican international air route controller confirms our en route path and assumes flight-following responsibility. On the flight deck, the

pilots have turned the aircraft over to the autopilot, and it takes its guidance from the INS. The navigator, Klindt, lays out his area chart and plots in key turn points. We'll be flying mainly a random series of courses concentrated over international waters between Cuba and the Yucatan Peninsula, one of the choke points of the

Wearing Coast Guard orange, Commander Kirk Colvin, the operations officer of the Clearwater USCG Air Station, monitors his flight instruments while on patrol over the Gulf of Mexico.

drug runs, as well as patrolling a sizable section of the Gulf of Mexico adjoining the passage. Steve Klindt is unique, not within the Coast Guard but within Herk crews. He is an enlisted navigator, the Air Force and Navy assigning commissioned officers to that position. The Coasties, in keeping with their limited personnel resources, train a select group of their aviation technicians to operate the INS and Omega systems and perform other basic navigational duties. After all, we have little black boxes for the major work now, and Klindt is well skilled in the preflight alignment and in-flight operation of the C-130 navigational systems. Ferreira, the radioman, is busily checking out his various radio circuits. Deglau eases back his flight engineer's ''throne'' and enters some engine and system readings into his log. The pilots relax in semireclined positions, their bodies cradled in sheep's wool as they keep an alert scan working the blue skies around them and the even bluer gulf below. They make small talk while monitoring the subtle inputs of the autopilot. The air is calm and clear, visibility certainly in the thirty to fifty mile range. Back aft, the two scanners, Turner and Lanning, having no search responsibilities at the moment, catch up on national and local happenings with the Sunday paper. The large windows at their stations provide plenty of light.

At 0955, the quiet ride is over. We cancel our IFR flight plan with Merida control — it is no business of theirs as to where we will go next — and drop out of 25,000 for our 1,600-foot initial search altitude. Colvin and Finnell erect their seats slightly and start a visual surface scan in earnest. Klindt adjusts and searches the multicolored radar return on his navigational scope. Unfortunately, the radar is weather ori-

ented and will not be as valuable to the search as the set programmed to be installed in the near future, particularly since our patrol today is looking at small stuff. Deglau plugs in the electrically powered, gyro-stabilized search glasses. Ferreira lays out his ship and boat rigging logs. Turner and Lanning put away their papers and adjust their position before their viewing windows. For the next five hours every surface craft that is within our visual and radar range will be examined. On each one, we will drop down to whatever altitude is necessary to detect their name and home port and examine their open decks. Their course and speed will also be reported.

At 1,600 feet, the Hercules zaps along like a heavy fighter, ground speed not too far from 300 mph, and we cover a lot of area fast. Only minutes after descending we pick up our first contact.

Colvin takes over manually and swings around to approach the contact from the stern. Several small vessels appear. We've run across a fishing covey, probably Mexican, with a small mother ship and several working boats. We pass close aboard the starboard side of the mother ship about a wingspan above the water, and Klindt and our port scanner, Turner, give the boat a good visual examination. The boatmen pay us little mind and nothing looks suspicious.

Fifteen minutes later another target appears ahead at about 10 o'clock, a single small ship. Deglau presses the gyro-stabilized glasses to his eyes and reads off the characteristics of the vessel.

Small cargo vessel . . . orange hull, green waterline, kingpost forward, green containers on deck, small superstructure aft, single funnel and mast. . . .

Colvin takes the Herk right down to the water

and we parallel the vessel's course, approaching from aft and to port. As we pass, Finnell reads off the markings on the side.

Bermuth Lines . . . didn't catch the name or port.

Lanning, back at the starboard scanning window, adds his evaluation.

Bermuth Lines . . . got pictures.

Finnell chimes in again with course and speed and Ferreira completes his log entries. We pull back up to search altitude.

And so it goes for the next five hours, search and detect, descend and identify. I begin to appreciate the presence of the adjustable seats with the plush sheep's-wool coverings. Fatigue and boredom can devastate alertness and efficiency. For a while I wonder how the crew can really tell if a vessel is suspicious; then I recall the story Pat Danaher related to me on our training flight.

You sort of develop an instinct. There may not be any obvious signs. But something may not look just right. We spotted one small craft while on patrol a while back that didn't seem to have any obvious reason for being where he was. He wasn't a fisherman and had no capacity for any great cargo. We came up on the radio and talked to him, and he identified his boat and stated he was in transit from point A to point B . . . had a slight Spanish accent . . . nothing suspicious about that. However, when we asked him his home port and registration, he came back with Monrovia, Liberia. Now, tankers and large cargo vessels may be registered in Liberia, but none of the small stuff needs that kind of registration. We alerted a nearby surface unit . . . they closed, and two of the boatmen went over the side into a raft while the third poured gasoline over the deck and cabin. . . . He wasn't the brightest druggie and when he lit a match the whole thing exploded and hurled him into the air, severely burned. One of our people got on board in time to retrieve one large bundle of marijuana, and the rest went down with the boat. But we got the evidence and the crew.

We're not so effective on this Sunday. A fair amount of surface traffic but nothing suspicious. Colvin calls Havana Control and files his IFR flight plan as we conclude our search and climb toward our requested back-home altitude. A female voice in Havana Center clears us back to Clearwater via the jet route structure and we level once more at flight level 250.

Colvin and Finnell express their disappointment.

Wonder where all the bad guys are.
Church?
Probably so. . . .

Within an hour we pass over Key West and skirt down the west side of the Florida peninsula, descending as we near the Tampa-St. Petersburg-Clearwater area. At 1650, Colvin eases the Herk back onto the Clearwater runway and we run through the Herk wash on the way back to the pad. We've picked up a lot of sea salt on our low passes and the wash keeps down the corrosion.

We shut down at 1710. Flight time — 8.6 hours. Routine — and we got off light.

I leave Colvin filling out postflight forms in the duty office. He still has several hours of work left. Some flight changes have come in while we were out ("Get the Coast Guard to do it!").

Me? I'm ready for a cool brew.

Chapter 8
Reserves and Air Guard

The heavy desert air parts violently as the bulb-nosed C-130B bulls its way headlong at close to 300 miles per hour, so low over the scrub grass that tiny creatures burrow deeper into the hot sand in a frantic effort to escape the synchronous roar of four turboprops at military power. The Hercules jinks sharply to the right, then half-rolls rapidly into a screeching left turn, losing even more altitude as it fights to keep enemy ground troops from laying on a successful fire-control solution. Then, it jumps up a hundred feet, groans through a gut-wrenching reversal, and scoops to the top of the grass before sweeping upward to a 500-foot drop altitude. For an awful moment, the pilot must keep the aircraft reasonably steady while two stacked pallets of weapons and provisions are jerked out of the open rear by the sharp pop of their khaki cargo chutes. A dozen Special Forces troops plunge headlong out of the open rear and follow the cargo drop onto the desert floor. As the last figure clears the lip of the opened ramp, the Hercules pulls up into a maximum performance climb, leans over al-

U.S. Air Force Reserve Hercules participate in airlift operations on an equal basis with regular forces.

most on its back, and opens toward the setting sun. Elapsed time since it appeared low on the horizon — ninety-three seconds.

At the controls, hunched in the command pilot's seat, is a thirty-two-year-old pharmacist; to his right, anxiously scanning his available piece of sky for signs of the bad guys, is a Colorado cattle breeder. The flight engineer, a full-time precision machinist, sits strapped to his throne between and slightly behind them, and is busily checking his engine and system instruments. The slightest irregularity and he will inform his pilot and start to troubleshoot the problem. Ninety-eight percent of the time, he'll solve it before his pilots can generate concern.

Back in the now-empty cargo cavern, the two loadmasters are securing their seat belts after transferring from their stations precariously near the lip of the loading ramp, which was closed immediately after the last paratrooper cleared the aircraft. One of them is a bit queasy despite his full-time profession as a high school gym instructor. The rapid series of positive and negative g's and violent roll maneuvers has churned the remnants of his box lunch within his stomach and threatens the tranquility of his upper gastric system. The other loadmaster, considerably older, just leans his forty-two-year-old spine back

A C-130B of the 731st TAS (Tactical Airlift Squadron) out of Peterson AFB, Colorado, airdrops with the best of them, routinely flying missions in CONUS and overseas.

against the nylon web of his troop seat and exhales deeply. He's getting a bit old for this type of big plane aerobatics, but none of his squadron mates would dare his wrath by suggesting the twenty-four-year aircrew veteran use the prestige of his E-9 stripes to assign himself a less strenuous job. His civilian role as dock foreman for a leading building supply company is already too soft for a man of his experience. Besides, he's already fought two full-fledged wars; this week-long excursion into a minor fracas is duck soup.

What's going on? Civilians executing a military strike? Not exactly. True, a covert team has just been placed on hostile soil by a pharmacist, a cowboy, a machinist, a high school gym coach, and a civilian dock foreman. And just

seventy-two hours back, they were all recipients of an urgent phone call, one which offered them the opportunity to "go flying." But civilians? Sort of; they are all members of today's professional Air Force Reserve (AFRES).

AFRES Tactical Airlift

Peterson Air Force Base sits on the high Colorado plains just at the base of the Rocky Mountains. The shared military-civilian airfield is at an elevation of 6,172 feet, and on this warm late-summer morning the temperature is eighty degrees. A light breeze flows off the mountains and sweeps across the seventeen C-130B aircraft assigned to the 731st Tactical Airlift Squadron (TAS) stationed at "Pete Field." The squadron is an integral part of 302d Tactical Airlift Wing (TAW), which is also a tenant activity on Peterson Air Force Base and in turn a unit of the 4th Air Force (headquarters, McClellan Air Force Base in California). The 731st is typical of the fifteen Air Force Reserve tactical airlift squadrons.

Inside the modern red brick building that houses the 731st offices, I walk into the squadron briefing room and am met by 1st Lt. Andy Redmond, USAFR, a smiling, big-boned Herk driver originally from Oklahoma City. A graduate of the Air Force Academy, Andy is now an ART (air reserve technician) and has been assigned to the 731st since January 1987. He needs only a few more flights to become tactically qualified, and today I'm going along on one of his training hops. He introduces me to the aircraft commander, Maj. Bob Buckhout, and the rest of the crew — Capt. R. G. Wengler, navigator; Sgt. Bruce Pyle, flight engineer; and the two loadmasters, Sergeants Clark Baker and Clinton Oliver. Ours will be a two-plane low-level drop mission, and we take our seats alongside the other crew as the briefing begins. In addition to being a training flight for Andy Redmond and a practice drop mission, the flight will include a tactical check for the navigator and an upgrade check for Major Buckhout.

The operations and navigations brief take only a few minutes. We're going to stay low and take the West 1 route to the drop zone near Yoder, Colorado, a small, rural community some twenty-eight miles east of Colorado Springs, drop a ''heavy'' palletized load, then swing around for another run, relinquishing the lead at that time to the other Herk, and make a CDS drop. After that, the aircraft will proceed to Red Devil, a forward area strip on the massive Fort Carson (Army) training range, which runs from Colorado Springs south. A piece of cake.

Weather is CAVU and there's just time to grab a sandwich before we meet at the aircraft. Andy Redmond, my cheerful guide, needs a refueling before the over-noon flight and we stop by the Operations snack bar. As he hungrily devours his cheeseburger, we sit and talk.

I'm trying to check out as a tac copilot but our operational commitments sometimes make it difficult to get the necessary training flights in — we fly quite a bit. I'll get around to it, of course . . . I've already taken the written, two months ago, so I'm getting anxious. Today should be a good flight — we've got plenty of training worked in.

I went to pilot training from the Academy and then right to C-130s. We fly a lot here. I get more flight time than my buddies, who are still on active duty. . . . Gosh, I've been running

Load 'em up and move 'em out! The cry of the Old West still lives in the attitude of the Colorado reservists of the 302d TAW (Tactical Airlift Wing), headquartered in Colorado Springs.

behind all day . . . I wolfed down my breakfast . . . shouldn't eat all this but it's the best deal going.

I have to agree, considering the small price of the daily special — cheeseburger, fries, and drink for $2.25. Andy glances at his watch and decides we're too close to ramp time. He finishes the cheeseburger and dumps the remaining fries into the trash receptacle.

We join the crew in the cargo compartment of Summit 02 and Major Buckhout supervises his crew briefing. In typical air force fashion it is thorough. No questions. I take my assigned seat on the lower seat-bunk on the flight deck. Strapped in next to me is 1st Lt. Doug Abbotts, the 302d TAW's enthusiastic chief of public af-

fairs and my official escort for the ride. Doug is not a pilot and knows that ahead of him lie several hours of low-level bouncing and jousting with some pretty hard-g evasive maneuvers at the completion of each drop. On a warm summer day, it can be uncomfortable, and he smiles gamely as we taxi out. This is part of his job.

After the mandatory engines and system checks, we roar down the runway. The warm temperature has adjusted the 6,000-foot elevation of the runway to a density altitude of just over 9,000 feet, and the Hercules recognizes only the higher figure in its reach for the sky. We take a few seconds longer than normal to reach our takeoff speed, but as soon as we're airborne with the wheels tucked away and the flaps up, the Hercules is ready for action. Buckhout banks right and we skirt around the field until we are clear of the traffic pattern, then drop to our 300-foot mission altitude. It will vary during the next two hours, somewhat lower as we speed across the rolling terrain, somewhat higher as we position ourselves for the drops.

I watch the Colorado countryside speed past as Buckhout flies under the navigational direction of Redmond and Navigator Wengler. At about two wingspans above the ground, horizon visibility is considerably less than at normal cruising altitudes. Landmarks appear only a few minutes before you reach them and at close to 300 miles per hour they appear, zap by, and disappear with alarming speed. Precision navigation is a function of constant attention to everything you can see

and is a team effort by everybody on the flight deck. Out here in the Colorado outback, some terrain features such as streambeds and washes change annually with the summer gullywashers, and charts don't always reflect their current shapes. Some studied interpretation is necessary — just as it would be if we were low-leveling across some unfamiliar European terrain with outdated charts. Good simulation. Andy has his WAC (World Aeronautical Chart) spread across his lap and is dead reckoning us along the West 1 route. Wengler is supervising by frequent glances at his own chart, timing our legs and keeping an avionics backup on our position. Of course, looming off to the west in this sparkling clear sky is Pikes Peak, so even I can keep track of where we are, generally.

I figure the Colorado citizens who live out here in the high plains are a pretty tolerant lot. While we scrupulously avoid flying right over the ranch houses, easing right or left to keep just outboard, the noise of a Herk passing just a few hundred feet away and at several hundred knots must cause a few country souffles to collapse. However, the cattle and horses don't even bother to look up, their nonchalance evidence of the frequency with which low-level flights pass their way. Just a bit to the east, over more sparsely settled land, are the B-52 and the B-1 training routes.

I listen on the intercom to the litany of chatter between Buckhout, Redmond, and Wengler as we approach the drop zone.

"Is that the tower we're looking for?"

"No . . . keep on going."

"Two minutes out of turn point . . . heading will be three-one-three degrees for forty-one miles."

"If it'll fit, we'll fly it" seems to be the motto of C-130 crews. You name it, and somewhere some Hercules has probably delivered it.

"Rog . . . tower at two o'clock."

"Lookit . . . ducks! What are ducks doing out here?"

"Look at 'em take off!"

"Hooooo, hooooo, watch out, big birdies. . . ."

"We're clear."

"There's the dry lake bed . . . where's the road?"

"That's it . . . up ahead."

"The map says it turns ninety degrees. That's not ninety degrees."

USAFR loadmasters position cargo pallets for a practice drop near Limon, Colorado.

"That's the road . . . there's the intersection."

"Got it. That's it."

"And there's the streambed . . . let's start the turn now."

We bank sharply and swing around to the left. Our wing Hercules, just behind and to the right of us, performs a gentle S turn, keeping station on us without having to change his power settings.

"Twenty-minute warning to drop."

"Loadmaster . . . got it."

"Rolling out on three-one-three degrees."

"We're a few seconds behind."

"I'll add a couple knots."

A few minutes later we're on our drop run. Buckhout eases the Hercules up to 7,150 feet — we're 1,050 feet AGL (above ground level).

I hurry aft to observe the drop. The "heavy" has been untied and positioned by the loadmasters. With an audible crack, the drogue chute streams and the pallet of cargo is jerked from the cargo compartment and drops almost out of sight. I watch the cargo chutes lower it gently onto the ground. Buckhout rolls sharply into an evasion maneuver and we descend for our low-level egress from the DZ.

"Hey! Good drop!"

"Right on."

"I figure a couple hundred over."

"No way. Good drop."

We watch the trailing Herk drop his heavy. Then, as we swing around for another approach, our companion takes the lead and we fly a loose trail position. Once again we steady on the run, this time only 500 feet AGL and the container delivery system (CDS) does its thing. I watch the drop and it looks good to me. We climb and head back toward Pete Field. My escort, Doug Abbotts, is a bit pale, but he still has his smile. The young man is dedicated to his work, but I have a distinct feeling he would rather be in Philadelphia.

The mission has gone like a piece of cake, indeed. And no reason for it not to. The crew is experienced and current. Captain Wengler is a veteran of the ill-fated Iran hostage rescue attempt and I am to learn later that Major Buckhout is a veteran Hercules jock with arctic experience in the skied birds of the New York Air National Guard. Therein lies much of the strength of the reserve squadrons. The crew members, particularly those full-time reservists designated as ARTs, stay in one job in one place much longer than their active-duty contemporaries. They develop a finely honed ability in their jobs.

The 731st is commanded by Lt. Col. Jim Folsom, and the wing commander is Col. Joe L. Campbell. Both officers are veteran Hercules aircraft commanders and very typical of the leadership of the Air Force Reserve units. Folsom is a twenty-five-year veteran of the USAF/AFRES, with 263 combat hours in Southeast Asia. A native of Ardmore, Oklahoma, colonel-selectee Folsom came to his prestigous command of the 731st TAS by way of extensive airlift flying duty and previous command. A 7,000-hour-plus pilot, he flies with TWA in his civilian life. Colonel Campbell, another native Oklahoman, became an air force officer by way of the AFROTC program at Baylor University and won his wings in 1961. He is a career-long airlift pilot, having cut his teeth on the magnificent flying machine the Douglas C-124 Globemaster. An ART since August 1966, Campbell was recalled to active duty in 1968 during the *Pueblo* crisis, and then returned to his ART duty in C-130Bs as a Herk squadron commander.

The 302d TAW includes 943d Tactical Airlift Group (TAG) at March Air Force Base in California, the 96th Mobile Aerial Port Squadron at Little Rock Air Force Base in Arkansas, and the 929th Civil Engineering Squadron at Lowrey

Air Force Base in Colorado. One of the newest airlift wings, the 302d is part of a Hercules reserve force that provides 26 percent of the USAF tactical airlift, 28 percent of the weather reconnaissance capability, 22 percent of aerospace rescue and recovery assets, 50 percent of AC-130 gunship forces, and 100 percent of air force aerial spraying capability. Reserve crews operate 158 C/AC/HC/WC-130 Hercules aircraft, and air reserve personnel (operating all types of aircraft), along with the men and women of the Air National Guard (ANG), constitute 24.1 percent of total air force forces (1987 figure).

The ART program itself deserves a few words of explanation, for it is the instrument with which the Air Force is able to train and keep its reserve Hercules components (as well as all its reserve units) at such a high state of readiness. ART applicants become wearers of two hats. As military personnel, they operate within the air force definition of their specialties and carry reserve grades and ranks; as civilians, they perform as full-time civil service employees at designated GS and WG levels, and are paid at those levels. In some of their duties they are sergeant or captain, and in others they are mister or miss/missus. The ART program allows the reserves to manage the Air Force Reserve forces. The 731st, then, is really a full-time minisquadron, which can fly daily missions if need be and is augmented on drill weekends and periods of active duty with the inactive reserves assigned to it. The ARTs train the part-timers and provide the continuity and proficiency level necessary to make at least a portion of the squadron instantly available during the first stages of mobilization. The 302d TAW employs more than 200 ARTs, and its full complement includes 900 reservists.

In keeping with the ART concept, the Hercules of the 731st range the world in their assigned tasks. A recent example is the 1987 deployment of 250 members of the 302d TAW, including aircraft and flight crews of the 731st TAS, to England for seventeen days of intensive training and operations. Missions were flown not only within England but also to Rhein-Main Air Base in West Germany, and then on to bases in Italy, Crete, and Denmark. The Colorado reservists performed alongside regular forces in an impressive display of readiness and proficiency. In the spring of 1988 the high-country airlifters were deployed south to support the U.S. Southern Command, operating out of Panama into South and Central American countries.

The men and women of the 731st are proud of their accomplishments as a team of full-time (ARTs) and part-time reservists. You can wander out on the flight line and pick almost anyone at random and find that (1) they are Herk enthusiasts and (2) they are good at what they do. Typical is T. Sgt. Ronald L. Martin, a qualified C-130 crew chief, a nineteen-year military veteran and a plank owner in the 731st, having joined the squadron in 1982 when it was established at Peterson AFB. A WG-11 grade civil servant in the ART program, Martin and one of his reservists, Senior Airman Kevin Logan, are catching their breath on the flight deck of one of the squadron Herks when I join them. Both wear big grins whenever they talk about the C-130, Martin eagerly singing the praises of the aircraft.

Terrific airplane — I've flown in them for over four years, three as a crew chief. We rarely miss a flight due to down time and they are old birds. We have some corrosion problems we have to keep on top of — some of them are Vietnam vets — but we have outstanding maintenance people.

Logan nods agreement. It's obvious he enjoys learning his skills under the veteran tutorship of crew chief Martin.

Both men are in an administrative chain of maintenance operations that has Sen. M. Sgt. Joe Campau as the 302d's maintenance control supervisor. Having joined the wing in 1985 as quality assurance chief, Campau brings to the Herk team a ten-year background in gunships and is an admitted buff of the aggressive fire-fighting member of the Hercules family.

I did four years active duty prior to becoming an ART — in C-141s part of the time — then became involved in the gunship operations down at Eglin and Hurlburt . . . we did a lot of things other than gunship missions. A fighter jock ejected over the water and we joined the search. The seas were rough and he was hard to find

---

A Hercules drops and slams onto a dirt strip. An assault team emerges, ready to fight. All in a day's work for the Air Reserves.

Fire-fighting Herks

In the summer of 1987, more than 1,250 fires raged across the wooded hills of California, and Herk rushed to put on its fire-fighting hat. Reserve units of the USAF Hercules force joined with their active-duty and Air National Guard comrades in a massive effort to contain the flames and reduce damage to property and the environment. The 943d TAG reservists from March Air Force Base were in the thick of the fight, installing modular airborne fire-fighting systems within the C-130 cargo bays and making repeated low-level flights into the turbulence and smoke that threatened to overcome fire-fighting efforts. On each flight, they dumped up to 3,000 gallons of Phoschek chemical, which gives flora some resistance to combustion. The reddish brown solution — a thick, syrupy liquid — also serves a second purpose, providing the soil with nutrients and other fertilizers to stimulate regrowth. Operating out of the refueling airports at Van Nuys and Fresno, the Herks of the 943d flew from dawn to dusk daily, wending their way across the hazardous terrain and trying to avoid the thick smoke. Drop altitudes were an extremely low 150–200 feet at airspeeds of 140 miles per hour, and each plume of chemical bathed a swath 150 feet wide and 2,000 feet long. The low-speed handling characteristics of the C-130 were never more tasked than during the fire-fighting effort.

Air National Guard

In addition to tactical airlift squadrons, the AFRES operates an AC-130A gunship squadron (711th SOS, Duke Field, Eglin Air Force Base);

If you can't stomp it out, call the Herks of the 943d Tactical Air Group, California fire fighters who deliver the big orange blob.

but we found him with our IR [infrared] . . . there he was, a warm dot on the cold ocean. Another time, there was a train wreck and we used our sensors to track a potentially dangerous toxic cloud that came from the wreck. We also flew range clearance flights prior to the space shuttle launches. Came here in 1985 and this is a great place to be with the Herks — but I miss the gunship duty. It was fun . . . we did a lot of things, many of them humanitarian rather than military.

Campau is half of an ART family. His wife, Rosemary, a master sergeant and a plans and scheduling technician, works just two doors down the hall from his office.

a WC-130H weather recco squadron (815th WRS, Keesler Air Force Base in Mississippi); and three HC-130H/N Aerospace Rescue and Recovery Squadrons (301st ARRS at Homestead Air Force Base in Florida, 305th ARRS at Selfridge Air National Guard Base in Michigan, and the 304th ARRS at Portland International Airport in Oregon).

The Hercules of the Air National Guard rival those of the Air Force Reserve in their high usage and versatility. A case in point is the New York Air National Guard crews, who fly skied C-130Hs and have the responsibility for logistic support of our arctic DEW Line stations. Since the advent of our early warning satellites, the support of the DEW Line radars has become a matter of insuring that they continue in a ready status as our early warning backup system. Originally supported by skied C-130Ds of the regular Air Force, then by commercial carriers, the DEW Line stations now receive regular resupply flights by the New York Herks flying out of Schenectady airport. As previously mentioned (Chapter 6), the C-130Hs of the New York ANG (179th TAS) are also being considered for deployed duty as search and rescue standby aircraft in Christchurch, New Zealand, for the Navy's austral winter flights to Antarctica.

The 193d Electronic Combat Group (ECG), an Air National Guard unit out of Harrisburg, Pennsylvania, provided a psyops Herk, an EC-130E Coronet Solo II aircraft, to the Grenada URGENT FURY operation (see Chapter 3). An interesting note concerning the 193d ECG is that while MAC is the gaining activity of the AFRES and other ANG Hercules units, the 193d's mobilization billet is with the Tactical Air Command.

Paralleling regular and reserve C-130 commit-

Brand new LC-130H skibirds of the New York Air National Guard will enhance logistic support of defense installations in Greenland and the Arctic.

ments, the Air National Guard also tasks its Hercules for Aerospace Rescue and Recovery Service (the 102d ARRS of the 106th ARRG of the New York ANG at Suffolk County Airport and the 129th ARRS, 129th ARRG, of the California ANG at Moffett Field Naval Air Station, both units flying the HC-130H models).

Along with their regular and reserve contemporaries, ANG squadrons fly the A, B, E, and H models (including a number of variants), although the two older series of Herks, the As and Bs, are gradually being phased out. Considering the normal sequence of events, the Air National Guard, as well as the regular and reserve Air Forces, can look forward to continued usage of the durable Hercules well into the twenty-first century.

Chapter 9
The Family Tree — and Other Offspring

The Hercules genealogist soon learns that some of the boughs of the C-130 tree are about to break with the weight of the number of variants that have proliferated since the birth of mama and papa back at Burbank. And it would seem that there are additional versions of the versatile and adaptive C-130 being devised almost daily. Thus far, we have confined our discussion to the major models and their more popular modifications. But what about the likes of the JC-130A, the NC-130E, the VC-130H, the MC-130E-S, or the JHC-130H?

In all, there have been more than fifty *major* versions just in the U.S. To look at all of them would involve an *Encyclopedia Britannica*–sized set of books.

Basically, a Herk is a Herk is a Herk, with some Herks perhaps a bit more Herky than others. Figure 1 shows the lineage and Appendix I identifies each of the major versions. So we'll confine our in-depth look to several of the more interesting modifications.

The wart-nosed DC-130 drone carriers are but one of the many variants of the Hercules, most civilian crewed but militarily employed.

We have to start with the Royal Air Force's Hercules W.Mk2 XV208. Originally a 1967 standard RAF C.Mk1 (Lockheed C-130K Serial No. 382–4233), the aircraft was operated as part of the Far East RAF until 1971. Then, during 1972–73 it was extensively modified by Marshall of Cambridge (Engineering) Ltd. Its most prominent feature is its Pinocchio nose, formed by the installation of a seven-meter-long protuberance that houses scientific instruments requiring exposure to undisturbed air. The brightly banded red and white boom preempts the nose installation of the regular weather and navigation radar, which has been relocated in a teardrop housing on top the fuselage aft of the overhead cockpit windows.

As an advanced meteorological research airplane assigned to the Meteorological Research Flight (MRF) division of the Royal Aircraft Establishment (RAE) in Farnborough, Hampshire, the special Hercules has ranged over the entire globe in a concentrated investigation of our meteorological environment.

In 1974, it took part in GATE (GARP Atlantic Tropical Experiment; GARP is Global Atmospheric Research Program — got all that?), the first of a number of international efforts to understand our weather systems. In 1978, the aircraft participated in JASIN (Joint Air-Sea Interaction) North Atlantic exercise; in 1981, it flew in the KONTUR (German-Konvection Turbulenz) program in the North Sea; and in 1985, it operated in support of the North Norway PLEXUS (Polar Low Experiment Using Sondes) operation. As recently as 1987, the unique Hercules spent a month in San Diego studying the processes involved in the formation and dispersion of low-level cloud sheets (believe me, you don't even want to know the acronym of that one). In late 1987, the W.Mk2 XV208 operated in its own backyard, flying the southwest approaches of the British Isles as it made microphysical measurements within active cold fronts. The released dropsondes descended through the various temperature, pressure, and wind force levels.

The list of scientific equipment within the interior of the aircraft is extensive and constantly changing according to the specific missions flown. Included are devices to determine basic meteorological variables such as horizontal and vertical winds, humidity, and pressure. There is an extensive aerosol and cloud physics set of instrumentation, including such valuable devices as an integrating nephelometer (samples aerosol

Figure 1   C-130 Derivatives

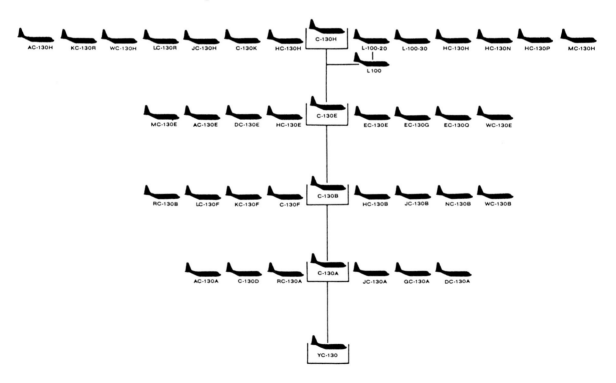

light scattering), a Pollak counter (particle concentration), and a cloud condensation nucleus counter. Chemical sampling of atmospheric components such as sulfur and nitrogen compounds, ozone, trace gases, and even liquid water (clouds) can be made. Various radiometers such as a pyranometer, pyrgeometer, and radiation thermometer measure an entire spectrum of broad-band, wide- and narrow-angle, and long- and short-wave radiation.

Cloud physics studies at such institutions as Oxford University and several high technological laboratories within England are supported by the RAE's meteorological flights.

Through it all, the British Hercules, dubbed ''Snoopy'' by its crews, retains its identity as a Lockheed C-130 with speed, range, and altitude capabilities, along with a cavernous cargo compartment for the installation of instrumentation, typical of the species. In service now for more than thirteen years, the picturesque Herk is one of a kind and will serve the RAE well into the next century.

The United States operates a similarly tasked WC-130, crewed by civilians of the National Oceanic and Atmospheric Administration (NOAA). While not as radical in appearance or as sophisticated in instrumentation as the British variant, the NOAA Hercules operates out of the agency's research center in Miami and also assists in hurricane plotting. Other tasks have included a hail-suppression program in Colorado and participation in a joint NASA/NOAA project to test new radar and laser ocean-wave sensors for subsequent use in sea-watching satellites. The NOAA WC-130 also ranges worldwide in its research flights.

The National Aeronautics and Space Adminis-

NASA's Earth Survey 2 Hercules ranges worldwide in its examination of our planet and the gases that surround it.

tration (NASA) operates another unique variant from the standpoint of mission. Civilian crewed, their NC-130B Hercules fulfills an earth survey role, developing techniques for subsequent remote satellite sensing. Prior to its NASA assignment, the Hercules (number seven off the B-model production line) was used by Lockheed in the early 60s for a STOL (short field takeoff and landing) research project, which involved installation of a boundary layer control modification. A pair of T-56 turbojet engines were hung below the wing, one on each side outboard of the regular engines, and used to provide ducted air across the wing to generate additional lift at slow speeds. The project produced some impressive results, the most notable of which was the lowering of takeoff and landing speeds into the

The Pinocchio-nosed W.Mk2XV208 RAF Hercules carries a host of sophisticated meteorological investigative equipment including delicate atmospheric probing devices within its red and white striped proboscis.

50–70-knot range from the normal 80–100-knot range.

Several major variant proposals never made it off the drawing boards but are worth looking at briefly, since they are excellent examples of the wide range of Hercules modification made possible by such a truly classic design.

First, there is the Hercules-on-Water (HOW) proposal. Involving the substitution of an amphibious hull version of the pressurized Hercules fuselage and the simple expedient of placing the engines on top of the wing (à la P-3 installation) rather than slung below, the HOW Herk concept had several promising features: an already proven airframe and wing; reliable and efficient turbo-prop engines; and a retractable twenty-one-foot hydroski, which extended ten feet down into the water until the Herk reached planing speed on its takeoff, thus improving rough-water performance. But there were other serious considerations, not the least of which was the virtual worldwide replacement of seaplanes by long-range, land-based aircraft. We didn't *need* a seaplane (the author's own opinion remains reserved), and further design changes were necessary. For example, water tests with a one-sixteenth-scale flying model indicated that the horizontal stabilizers might have to be relocated, since they could suffer damage on water takeoff and/or landing. Relocation would involve major redesign and engineering tests, and in the day of the disappearing seaplane, necessary funding was hard to come by. So the proposed 175,000-pound Sea Herk went the way of the earlier turbo-prop Consolidated R3Y seaplane — into oblivion. However, some die-hard Herk drivers within the skied-Hercules community still discuss the pros and cons of shooting water landings with their skibirds, and many a happy-hour conversation has been enlivened with such discussions ("Hell's bells, we have three skis; the Herk seaplane had only one!" "Right on!" "Let's write Lockheed — who's got a pencil?").

Initially, a more promising variation was the twin-engined Hercules, another drawing board proposal advanced as model L-400. After all, if the standard Herk was such a rugged, short-field, open-terrain airplane, why not a slightly smaller and lighter two-engined version for short hauls and commuter cargo delivery? There should be a military use also, perhaps forward area tactical transportation. The normal C-130 fuselage and empennage would be retained. The wing center section would be shortened, eliminating the inner flaps, and H-model outboard panels

The twin-engined mini-Herk never got beyond the model stage but the concept is still discussed. Newer technology could revive the idea.

with four-foot tip extensions would be affixed (total wing span: 119 feet). Engines would be Allison 501-D22Ds of 4,591 shaft horsepower each. Fourteen-foot-diameter automatic feathering propellers would be installed and the engines equipped for water-methanol injection.

The concept envisioned an 85,000-pound maximum gross weight aircraft that could still carry the same bulk cargo as the C-130 while limited to 25,000 pounds of cargo weight. It would be more economical to build and operate, using a two-man crew on the flight deck. Because the plane was lighter, one main wheel could be eliminated on each side.

But it soon became apparent that the smaller Herk would not be that much more tactically advantageous to the military than the standard Herk, which was already a proven design. In addition, the state of the national economy in the late 70s was such that it was doubtful that the civilian market for the L-400 would materialize. Consequently, in 1980, Herk's baby brother was placed on the back burner.

One major variant has become quite successful and is being extensively employed, however — the stretched Hercules. Initially a modification of the civilian L-100 series, the two stretch versions, the L-100-20 and the L-100-30, have entered the civilian air cargo business with minimum fanfare. The stretch Herk is a natural growth of the basic airplane and consists of two inserts in the fuselage.

The L-100-20 involves a total stretch of 100 inches, 60 inches aft of the flight deck and 40 inches aft of the wing, giving the L-100 a total cargo space of 5,307 cubic feet (as opposed to the 4,500 cubic feet of the standard L-100). The L-100-30 involved a 180-inch stretch, 100 inches behind the flight deck, 80 inches aft of the wing (cargo capacity increased to 6,057 cubic feet). With a cargo compartment 9 feet high by 10 feet wide by 55 feet long, the dash-30 easily takes two standard 8- by 8- by 20-foot containers (or one 40-foot-long container) plus one 10-foot-long container. With such a bulk capacity it is easy to see why the L-100 remains a success in the civilian cargo field (see Chapter 10).

The British early on recognized the value of the stretch to their military Hercules fleet by contracting with Lockheed-Marietta to convert thirty of its regular C-130s to the C-130H-30 configuration (180-inch stretch) and took delivery of the first one in December 1979. Subsequent stretch modifications have been undertaken in Great Brit-

ain by Marshall of Cambridge (Engineering) Ltd. The new models carry a Hercules C.Mk3 designator. The stretched configuration gives each aircraft a 128-combat troop capacity (vice 92 in standard C-130), a 92-paratrooper capacity (vice 64), and a 97-litter capacity (vice 74). While maximum payload has been decreased due to increased basic aircraft weight, actual cargo cube capacity has increased, as has the ability to carry more standard pallets (seven vice five). Recognizing this, Indonesia became the first Hercules operator to order new production C-130H airplanes, and delivery commenced in 1980.

The United States military is just beginning to order the C-130H-30, having observed in late 1987 a record airdrop at Fort Bragg of twenty-four CDS bundles, each with its own parachute, with a total rigged weight of 43,262 pounds. The Super Hercules also made a pass to drop a complete field artillery section consisting of an eight-foot pallet holding 7,710 pounds of ammunition, a sixteen-foot pallet upon which were strapped an M102 105mm howitzer weighing 7,260 pounds, a twenty-foot pallet holding an M561 Gamma Goat prime mover weighing 12,360 pounds, and an eight-man gun crew! The world record drop was made in one thirty-second pass.

The Lockheed pilot for the drop, Robert B. Hill, in the tradition of Stanley Beltz and Leo Sullivan, wore an ear-to-ear smile as he described how the Super Hercules performed, stating that the aircraft was stable in all modes and had slightly less drag due to its increased "fineness ratio." "Throughout the entire test," he stated, "the feel of the airplane was the same as the standard airplane."

The DC-130H drone-carrying Hercules is another example of the versatility of the basic C-130 design. Initially conversions of A and E models, the drone carriers have long been used to drop various types of remotely piloted vehicles (RPVs). During the Vietnam era, the USAF and the U.S. Navy used the DCs to launch photographic drones, decoy drones to locate SAM sites, and electronic "listening" intelligence-gathering drones. The RPVs were also flown back to their bases by drone pilots aboard the DC mother aircraft.

After the Southeast Asia conflict, the USAF laid on a more demanding specification for a DC conversion — the ability to carry and launch four 10,000-pound RPVs. Using the more modern H model, the conversion was made by strengthening the wing and extending the nose to accommodate tracking and telemetry instrumentation. The capacity of the aircraft's electric generators was increased and a command and control center with Loran radar-navigation equipment was installed in the cargo compartment. Large viewing windows were also installed to observe the four pyloned RPVs.

The pylons were "wet" and could be used to refuel the drones before launch. Consequently, the drones could actually be started before takeoff for slightly increased thrust. Finally, long-range tanks were installed in the unused portion of the cargo bay. The DC-130H set an unofficial world record when it became airborne with its four RPVs hanging below its wing, and the subsequent sixteen test flights were so successful that the aircraft was ordered to Edwards Air Force Base for operational testing. However, the Air Force failed to award a production contract for additional aircraft, possibly because of the advance of other more sophisticated systems (satellite intelligence gatherers, for example), and the

Twenty-four (count 'em—the last one is just coming out) pallets form a record drop for the latest Hercules, a C-130H-30. All within three seconds, yet.

DC-130 program has diminished, one remaining example being a civilian-operated drone carrier at the Pacific Missile Test Center in Point Mugu, California.

The evolution of the variants discussed above as well as a great number of less involved adaptions such as the Royal Saudi Arabian fleet of nine Hercules, each equipped with hospital facilities and some capable of supporting open-heart surgery, and the special command and control Hercules of the USAF, equipped with complete module command and control capsules, has demonstrated that the mighty Hercules can apparently do everything but reproduce itself — and some folks are beginning to wonder about that!

Chapter 10
Civilian Hercules

It is quite a normal thing for an aircraft to make the transition from civilian to military life. Witness the widespread use of civil transports as early military airlift vehicles: the DC-3 was drafted in the late 30s and early 40s as the C-47 Skytrain; the DC-4 put on its Army Air Corps uniform as a C-54 and was joined by its sleeker sister, the Lockheed C-121 Constellation; later on, the DC-6 donned air force fatigues as the C-118. In more recent years the Lockheed Electra has become a most successful navy long-range antisubmarine patrol aircraft, and there are numerous other examples.

But going the other way, from military design and intent to widespread civilian use, is almost unheard of except for the postwar conversion of military surplus aircraft, such conversions being mainly for ego trips rather than efficient commercial employment. There have been some outstanding useful exceptions, however — Jacques Cousteau's converted PBY, for instance, and the modification of the huge ex-navy Mars seaplanes as aerial fire fighters.

Smokey Heel, a legend in its own time, soars skyward from a snow-covered strip at Great Bear Lake, Northwest Territories. Look at that grin!

Then along came Hercules, and the Lockheed folks early on recognized that there was a hungry civilian market just waiting for such a bird. They felt that civilian requirements were slightly different, however, and came up with their model GL-207.

Proposed as a 250,000-pound lifter, with 6,000-shaft horsepower (shp) Allison T-61 engines, the C-130 modification would have a longer fuselage by twenty-three feet four inches (and thus larger cargo compartment) and an increased wingspan to insure an acceptable wing loading. Almost before the design ink was dry, Pan American and Slick Airways placed orders for 1962 deliveries. Encouraged, Lockheed design engineers came up with two additional, even more powerful, GL-207 proposals: a 230,000-pound gross weight aircraft powered by 6,400-shp Rolls Royce Tyne engines and a 250,000-pound gross weight version powered by 22,000-pound-thrust Pratt and Whitney JT3D-11 turbofan engines.

Regrettably, Pan Am and Slick reevaluated their orders and decided to cancel them. Lockheed was left with a tough decision: Should they continue with the promising but expensive GL-207 development or take another look at the basic C-130 design? They chose the latter course, modifying the Hercules slightly to obtain FAA certification and designating it their L-100 civilian model (the only noticeable exterior change was the elimination of the bottom cockpit windows). The wisdom of their decision was revealed when on its first flight, April 20, 1961, the first L-100 Herk flew for a record-breaking twenty-five hours and one minute!

Powered by Allison 501–22 engines, civil versions of the T-56, the L-100 received Federal Aeronautics Administration certification in February 1965. The following September, the first aircraft was delivered to Continental Air Services. Hercules had doffed its fatigues and put on its blue jeans.

Twenty-two L-100s (including the prototype) were produced. Nine were later rebuilt as L-100-20 stretched Herks and another pair became L-100-30 Super Herks (see Chapter 9 for dash-20 and dash-30 details).

The L-100-20 entered service with Interior Airways in October 1968, and a total of twenty-five production-line dash-20s were built.

The L-100-30 made its maiden flight in 1970, the first models going to Saturn Airlines that same year. The dash-30 has been the dominant L-100 production model ever since.

Much of the work performed by the L-100s parallels the tasks of the military "trash haulers": the transportation of anything and everything. The list of foreign and domestic airlines employing the L-100 changes frequently as new carriers come on the scene and older ones, for one reason or another, phase out of the cargo business. Delta Airlines, Alaska International Air, Pacific Western Airlines, Southern Air Transport, Air America, Pacific Western, Interior Airways, Transamerica, Markair, and Continental Air Service are just some of the names that have graced the sides of U.S. civilian Herks. Foreign registrations include such diverse nations as France (SFair), Australia (Cargomasters PTY, Ltd.), South Africa (SaFair Freighters), Zambian Air Cargo, United African Airlines, and Pakistan International Airlines. The list goes on and on. The most recent purchaser, the People's Republic of China (PRC), is now flying its first Herk in its national air cargo airline. The incredible ability of the Hercules to carry bulky cargo into the most demanding of areas has given it a very distinct civilian personality to go alongside its macho military image. And if we had to cite one example of that worldwide personality, it would be *Smokey Heel.*

That final production-line L-100 started off life as a hauler with Flying "W" Airways. Employment with Dodge Aviation came next, and subsequently the Herk with somewhat of a modest beginning was sold to Canada's James Bay Energy Corporation and became a heavy hauler, indeed. The sole air link with the corporation's massive hydroelectric project in northern Quebec, Hercules CF-DSX (Canadian registration) supported the 12,000-man construction crew with as many as twenty-four flights a day, carrying roughly 4,500 tons of freight every month. During this period, the Herk was leased to Echo Bay Mine, Ltd., and it soon became a living legend within the civilian Herk community. So impressed was Echo Bay with the Herk's superb airlift performance that they bought the airplane from the James Corporation. It was Echo Bay's intention to use CF-DSX from their base at Yellowknife to provide logistic support to their silver diggings at Port Radium, Northwest Territories, and to commence the construction of a gold mine

110

A hauler with class, MarkAir's stretched Super Hercules is typical of the civilian version of the C-130. Cost effective and reliable, more and more Herks will be seen in mufti.

at Lupin, 250 miles northeast of Yellowknife. Now, remember Herk fans, we're talking one airplane here. CF-DSX hauled in every nut, bolt, piece of steel, case of beer, and roll of toilet paper that were needed to construct the mine in addition to a thousand-ton-a-day ore crusher, smelter, offices, and support buildings (and later hauled every gold ingot out). Piloted primarily by a gent named Bob Benson (the chief pilot who came with the package when CF-DSX was purchased from the James Corporation) and with

the able participation of such people as Bill Granley, Echo's aviation manager, and Don Switzer, flying training manager, the mine company put together a team of flight crews that accomplished practically the impossible. Benson had more than thirty-four years of flying entered in his stack

111

In Nepal, an SFair L-100-20 swallows a helicopter for delivery to a remote site.

of pilot's logbooks and was a 10,000-hour Herk driver (that's right, four zeros). Other recruited pilots were all veterans of arctic flying, although not necessarily with previous C-130 experience. Shucks, any decent aviator could fly the C-130 with a proper checkout — it is a pilot's airplane — but it takes years to acquire arctic flying savvy.

The lone Hercules *Smokey Heel,* named after a Canadian bush pilot who was a legend in *his* own time, made its initial deliveries of a bulldozer and other airstrip-carving equipment by landing on the frozen ice of Contwoyto Lake (Lupin was

on its western shore). Later on, it used the 5,000-foot landing strip, adding another regular stop to its itinerary — the 4,800-foot gravel and ice strip at Port Radium. Temperatures were in the minus-fifty-degrees-and-below range, and severe crosswinds were not at all uncommon. The advent of winter was actually anticipated by the pilots with some joy, for the even colder temperatures would freeze over the lake, and there would be a five-foot-thick slab of ice to support their heaviest loads and provide them with a more suitable 8,000-foot-long iceway.

Within a twelve-month period (October 1980 to October 1981), *Smokey Heel,* the hard-hat Herk, logged 1,989 hours of airlift time and carried 47 *million* pounds of freight! Benson and his pilots eased the loaded Herk onto the tundra and the ice more than 2,000 times in the task. The Lupin mine was completed in about one-fifth the time it would have taken to bring in the equipment, buildings, and supplies by ground transportation.

In one of those ironic twists that so often seem to plague those who perform well, death claimed Bob Benson in the spring of 1983. He had lots of flying left, and there are those who feel that he is still adding entries to his ethereal logbooks, for on the nose of the fabulous CF-DSX the name *Smokey Heel* has given way graciously to *Bob Benson.*

A rugged aircraft for a rugged route. Northwest Territorial Airlines' L-100–30 plies the Canadian north and thrives on arctic operations.

With that record performance of CF-DSX now history, some movie company is certainly missing the boat on a film of the single Herk airlift that built the Lupin mine. Perhaps it is because John Wayne is gone, too, and who else could play the bigger-than-life Benson?

Currently, there are more than fifty civilian operators of the L-100 series worldwide, and together they employ just under two hundred Hercules. SaFair Freighters has the largest fleet, seventeen. Of course, with Lockheed still rolling three aircraft per month off their assembly line and sales still healthy, the numbers change practically monthly as well. The January 1988 edition of *Air Cargo Guide* indicates that the major cargo charter airlines utilizing the Hercules are Markair, Inc. (U.S.), SaFair Freighters (South Africa), Secmafer Aviation (SFair, France), Cargomasters PTY, Ltd. (Australia), and Southern Air Transport, Inc. (U.S.). A number of other scheduled airlines and smaller cargo lines also fly the L-100.

As you might expect, our neighbor to the north puts the Hercules to good use. The remoteness of many of its northernmost populated areas and the adverse effects of the cruel arctic winter on surface traffic make air transportation a viable link in the everyday life of the Canadians. Consider Northwest Territorial Airways (NWT).

Canada's seventh largest airline, NWT serves such far north communities as Coppermine, Holman Island, Cambridge Bay, Gjoa Haven, Spence Bay, Pelly Bay, and Iqaluit. Headquartered at Yellowknife International Airport, the thriving company is an outgrowth of a very small single-plane airline established by the now-president and chief executive officer, Robert P. Engle. His aircraft was a single-engined De Havilland Otter and his company consisted of two employees — Engle and a pilot engineer. Engle, himself a bush pilot who came to Yellowknife first in 1956 and again in 1958 to stay, brings to the leadership of NWT a lifetime of flying experience in the particular conditions of the far north and a history of airline management that is based on that experience as well as a business management degree from Yale University.

NWT's current inventory is five Lockheed Electras, five DC-3s, and one L-100-30 Super Hercules. The company Hercules delivers the heavier, bulkier cargo to the frozen tundra while the Electras are able to deliver the more compact cargo. The efficiency and reliability of the sisters-under-the-skin Electra-Hercules team have enabled NWT to expand its cargo operations into a profitable alliance with Air Canada. If anyone thinks that a one-Hercules cargo airline is small potatoes, then consider NWT when it was just a one-Otter airline. Management, performance, and growth are an often-quoted triad of successful business factors, and in the air cargo business, Hercules provides that vital middle ingredient.

Overseas, the work of Hercules is a source of worldwide admiration, particularly in the developing countries. The tiny nation of Gabon has dipped into its limited budget and purchased a lone Hercules. Handicapped by an inadequate surface transportation system, Gabon has seen its L-100 open new doors to national development, giving the country's 500,000 people a renewed hope for economic development. Herk carries cargo and people to every jungle community where there is an ample landing area; on one occasion it transported an entire supermarket from Libreville, Gabon's capital city, to a provincial community. Gabon's President Bongo flies often on the Hercules to visit personally with his constituents in remote areas and has been quoted as saying that "the Hercules is a great boon to our nation."

The Republic of Indonesia has used its Hercules of Pelita Air Service to transport more than 300,000 people in a national relocation effort to relieve overcrowding in Java and Bali, each L-100-30 flight carrying 128 passengers and their belongings.

Peru uses its Herks for oil and mineral exploration in its Amazon interiors, Chile and Colombia use theirs in an intensive program of development, and cattle are air-shipped between a number of South and Central American nations. Iran, Saudi Arabia, Egypt, Abu Dhabi and Morocco all operate the Hercules as a vital arm of their economic development.

Hercules, more than any other aircraft within the author's knowledge, is rapidly becoming the single most important factor in the role that aviation plays in the economic development of the emerging nations of the world. World passenger airlines certainly bring human expertise to the most remote corners of the globe and support an expanding commonality among world nations, but it is the Hercules that provides the versatility, flexibility, and reliability to do everything that can be expected of a civilian airlifter.

Witness the performance by a Transamerica L-100-30 (the company operates a fleet of twelve). Transamerica was faced with a task of delivering a five-million-pound oil rig to a mountainous jungle site 200 miles inland from the northern coast of Papua, New Guinea. In a two-month operation, flying three times a day, seven days a week, the Transamerica L-100 never missed a single flight due to mechanical malfunction. And all flights were on schedule. Phenome-

The first L-100-30 purchased by China Air Cargo awaits its ferry crew at Lockheed-Georgia's Marietta complex.

nal? No, merely *typical* of the performance of the mighty Hercules.

Overall, twenty-eight operators in twenty nations worldwide are flying the L-100-30. Add to that the nations flying the L-100 and L-100-20 series and you have fifty-eight foreign countries employing the Hercules in a civilian role.

In late 1987, China Air Cargo, a subsidiary of China's national airline (CAAC, Civil Aviation Administration of China), took delivery of their first of two dash-30s, which will form the core of their updated air cargo service. Chinese and Lockheed-Georgia officials greeted the delivery with undisguised enthusiasm. Said the PRC's ambassador to the United States, Ambassador Han Xu, "Today is a historic day for both China Air Cargo and for the Lockheed-Georgia Company. For China Air Cargo, it is the initiation of a program that will lead to significant air cargo routes throughout the Far East."

Gosh, can you imagine how many fortune cookies a dash-30 can carry?

Chapter 11
Foreign Usage

On the dark night of June 13, 1982, C-130H TC-65 *Cobre* slipped onto the ill-lighted and bomb-damaged strip at Port Stanley, East Falkland Island. It was the last blockade runner of the war and Capt. Hernan A. Daguerre of the Argentine Air Force breathed a quiet prayer of gratitude as his aircraft commander, Commodore R. F. Mela, air-braked the Hercules to a slow crawl and positioned it for the unloading of their cargo — a 155mm howitzer and eighty rounds of ammunition. As the gun crew struggled to off-load the heavy gun, the dark night became as bright as day as star shells fired by an offshore British warship illuminated the airport. It was the final hours of the conflict over the Falkland Islands.

Captain Daguerre felt his mouth go dry again. British Harriers were undoubtedly in the area; there was even a report that several of the spunky VTOL fighters had left their combat air patrol station over the British carrier group to the east and were heading toward Port Stanley. A Hercules stopped on the airfield under the awful glare of the flares was a doomed aircraft. Daguerre joined the other members of the crew in frantic egress and they ran for cover.

Strangely enough, the Harriers from the British 800 Squadron remained in an orbit off the beach for forty minutes and then left. The crew of *Cobre* returned to their aircraft. The off-loading was quickly finished and seventy-two sick and wounded comrades were placed on board. The Hercules lifted back into the early morning air and set its course for Commodora Rivadavia, its home base on the Argentine mainland. It was the final C-130 resupply flight of the war.

Argentina, taking an aggressive stand after years of claiming that the Falklands — the Islas Malvinas — were Argentine territory, had invaded and occupied the south Atlantic islands. The Hercules became a vital combatant on both sides, Argentina having acquired three C-130Es in 1968, and subsequently five C-130Hs, thus giving the 1st Brigade of the Argentine Air Force a small cadre of modern tactical airlift vehicles at the outbreak of the war. (Actually, seven Hercules were available, one of the E models having been lost in a prewar sabotage incident.) The Argentines also operated two KC-130H tankers.

The British, of course, had a sizable Hercules

Tunisia became the 56th country to operate the Hercules when it took delivery of its first C-130 in 1985.

A flashy dresser, this Indonesian Air Force C-130H-30 is typical of the stretched Hercules used by such nations as Thailand, Algeria, Cameroon, Dubai, Nigeria, and Saudi Arabia.

force — fifty-four aircraft, operated by Squadrons 24, 30, 47, and 70.

The Falklands encounter was a unique conflict, the battle area being only 500 miles from one of the adversaries, yet 8,000 miles from the other. While the short war involved army, naval, and air forces of both combatants, it is for the moment only the operations involving the Hercules that are of interest to us. And the diverse tactical deployment and employment of the two Hercules forces are interesting indeed. Imagine a World War II battle fought in the skies over Britain where both sides flew ME-109s — or Spitfires. Or Yanks and Japanese going at it over the Pacific, both in Hellcats — or Zeros. Such a fantasy gives a generic quality to air war — bad guys and good guys, all wearing the same color hats.

But, regretfully, the tragedy and horror are unaffected.

On a November morning I walk into the office of the Argentine liaison officer at Wright-Patterson Air Force Base in Dayton, Ohio, and am welcomed by Hernan Daguerre, now a major and more than five years removed from that hectic night flight into and away from Port Stanley.

His warm smile and firm grip are indicative of his eagerness to speak of the Hercules and the role it played in that fateful, short war. I present him with a gift, a British-authored account of the Falklands war wherein they recognize the heroic crews of the Argentine Hercules of the Grupo 1 de Transporte Aereo Escaudron 1 (Group 1 of Air Transport Squadron 1). The Brits write with unconcealed admiration, "If the claim can be made that the Sea Harriers above all other aircraft enabled Britain to win the Falklands war then it should be said, with equal conviction, that it was the FAA's [Fuerza Aerea Argentina — Argentine Air Force] C-130 Hercules fleet that enabled Argentina to make a fight of it!"

Our conversation is open and candid — just two Hercules pilots speaking of a common love. Daguerre laughs gently as he talks, the laughter a reflection of the good fortune that accompanied him on that last flight and a recognition of the tense yet humorous time that saw him running for his life one moment, then risking it once more for his comrades and country.

It was crazy . . . I was very scared. . . . It was a frightening thing to wait for the shells or the attack by the British Harriers.

He shakes his head at the wonderment of the fact that the Harriers never came. I admire his admission of fear, the mark of a true warrior.

Daguerre, of French extraction and a native of Buenos Aires, is a graduate of the Argentine Air Force Academy and their Air War College, graduating number one in his class at the latter. A veteran of 2,000 hours in the Hercules, he holds the rating of instructor pilot. Assigned to Wright-Patterson in July 1986, to coordinate logistic support of Argentine Air Force C-130s, he is on a two-year tour in the U.S.

After the Malvinas conflict I became an instructor pilot in the C-130. I have flown the C-47, also a good airplane . . . did you read the book by Colonel Moro?

When I respond that I have not, Daguerre opens a desk drawer and hands me a heavy paperback entitled *Historia del Conflicto del Atlantico Sur.* My Spanish is rusty but I have no trouble translating the title. I'll get through the book, too, although it will take me a while, and I appreciate Daguerre's way of insuring that I have both sides of the story.

Colonel Moro is very knowledgeable about the history . . . it is a very incredible book. . . . You will find the information objective. He's assigned now in Washington. . . . He was a C-130 pilot during the war . . . he collected lots of the information from the British people . . . the book has even the dates and names.

We talk about Argentina's antarctic stations and compare notes on operating the Hercules in that environment. It is an operation we have in common, and Daguerre allows that the C-130 is "fantastic" when it comes to antarctic flying. I certainly agree. For the next hour, we discuss the Malvinas C-130 operations.

Truly, the *Chanchas* — mother sows — of Argentina, as their C-130s were affectionately

Like bees around a jar of honey, Spanish Armada AV-8A V/STOL Harriers sip their special nectar from a Hercules tanker.

dubbed, did "make a fight of it." At the outbreak of Operation Rosario the Chanchas commenced their airlift in support of the amphibious landings by the armada. Throughout the conflict, the Argentine C-130s kept up a steady stream of resupply flights despite the forbidding winter storms and the damaged runway at Puerto Argentino (Port Stanley). Bomb craters denied them use of the full runway, and the arrival of British air in the area forced their resupply flights to be concentrated during hours of darkness. The crews had to fly at wave-top heights until popping up at Port Stanley for a nerve-racking approach, delaying the use of their landing lights until the last possible moment and in general ignoring the thirty-five-knot crosswind, eighty-meter ceiling, and four-kilometer visibility minimums specified for their missions. Their aerial bridge ("Puento Aereo") was maintained until the closing hours of the conflict, ending with Daguerre's departure in *Cobre* on June 14.

The Argentine KC-130Hs were equally tasked in aerial refueling operations; the Super Entardards that launched the HMS *Sheffield*-killing Exocet missiles had a long drink of Hercules-provided fuel before their attack. Argentine Skyhawks routinely made a refueling connection shortly after takeoff and another on their way home.

Skillful airmanship, alert tactics (using adverse weather, darkness, and low altitudes to avoid detection), and determination allowed the Hercules to operate unscathed, except for one instance when a C-130 was employed for aerial reconnaissance — a very uncharacteristic task and one for which the Herk is ill-suited in a combat environment — and was jumped by a pair of Harriers. The aircraft and crew were lost.

Daguerre's smile fades as he recalls the incident.

They should not have been used in such a way. The C-130 is defenseless . . . the Harrier pilots knew that. Of course, in war they had to do what was necessary. . . . It was very bad for my friends.

It is almost noon and Daguerre has a luncheon commitment. I excuse myself and we clasp hands. His smile returns but the bad memory remains in his eyes.

Although we supported the British in the Falklands conflict, I feel very close to the Argentine Herk driver, who graciously thanks me for listening to his story.

The British Hercules, twelve of which had received the stretch configuration by Marshall of Cambridge, were faced with an equally formidable task although strategically a quite different one. And the indomitable Englishmen met it with their traditional ingenuity and determination.

To provide tactical airlift support to their Falkland Islands task force, their C-130s had to fly first from Lyneham to Gibraltar and then to Ascension Island. From Ascension, the Hercules flew airdrop missions to the British fleet, delivering high-priority cargo to the ships underway for the south Atlantic. But even from Ascension, they could not reach the ships nearing the Falklands.

Using a pair of cylindrical internal fuel tanks originally installed in earlier Andover and Argosy aircraft, the British were able to extend the range of the Hercules by three to four hours; by installing four tanks, they provided an even longer range. Thus modified, the Herks were designated LR2 and LR4 models and deployed from Lyneham nonstop to Ascension Island.

On April 15, 1982, Marshall of Cambridge commenced modifying a number of C-130s for in-flight refueling, installing the reception probes on top of the fuselage just aft of the pilots' stations, offset slightly to starboard, and fairing in the plumbing necessary to route the fuel to the Hercules tanks.

Initially, the Hercules C1.Ps, as they were redesignated, refueled from a Victor K2, but the Victor's slowest safe speed was still a bit too fast for the Hercules at altitude, and refueling had to be accomplished during a shallow 500-fpm (feet per minute) dive.

The modification was a success, however, and the first refueled mission left Ascension Island, flew a 6,300-mile sortie, and airdropped a 1,000-

pound load plus eight parachutists to HMS *Antelope*. Later on, the Hercules were to be provided with a more suitable refueler, the Douglas KC-10.

Australia became the first foreign power to acquire the Hercules, purchasing twelve of the early C-130A production models in December 1968. Since then, the latest Lockheed accounting reports that another fifty-six foreign countries have added the Hercules to their military inventories.

Due to internal political changes the Hercules now finds itself in unfriendly hands as well. Iran, once the operator of the largest C-130 fleet outside of the U.S., remains the possessor of a sizable C-130 contingent, although the deterioration of crew expertise and lack of replacement parts have probably decimated their utilization. North Vietnam counts the Hercules among its spoils of war.

Saudi Arabia fields an impressive C-130 force, having acquired more than fifty Hercules over the years. Canada's air force inventory includes thirty-seven Herks. Fifteen countries boast a force of ten to twenty C-130s apiece.

Israel flies fourteen Hercules and counts among its most successful employment the July 1976 Entebbe raid, a daring yet classical use of the versatile tactical airlifter. Brigadier General Joshua Shani of the Israeli Air Force spoke in September 1987 to the cadets of the Air Force Academy in Colorado Springs of his admiration for the Hercules. General Shani flew the lead aircraft of the four Herks participating in the Entebbe raid. The force boldly flew into the civilian airport of that Ugandan city and rescued 103 Israeli citizens who were being held captive in the airport terminal. Shani, smiling at the personal implication of his words, stated during his Colorado visit that planes such as the C-130 can make a man's military career.

On the other side of the volatile political situation in the Middle East, the Arabic countries employ some fifty-six Hercules. Libya, as a case in point, has purchased sixteen Herks since their first C-130H acquisition in 1970.

In summary, considering both the military and civilian use of the Hercules, practically every major nation outside of the Soviet bloc has recognized the value of the C-130 and now employs the aircraft in the conduct of its political, economic, and military endeavors. It is an unprecedented testimonial to the durability and adaptability of the Lockheed design to the various requirements of countries spread all over the face of the earth.

A Hercules duo makes a low pass over Grand Junction, Colorado.

Chapter 12
Future Development

Carl A. Hughes sits by me at the lunch table in the Lockheed-Marietta plant cafeteria, munching on a plate of beef tips and noodles. I know of the man, but this is the first time I've met him, and my Lockheed hosts are treating me to lunch. I know Carl has a thousand tales, but discretion (a trait journalists are quite uncomfortable with) dictates that I be patient. The stories will come.

Hughes is the physical opposite of Leo Sullivan; small, more of a fighter pilot in stature, with the eyes of that breed. He, too, has been relegated from the cockpit to more mundane tasks, but certainly not mundane in their importance to the continued growth of the Hercules. Carl is a senior test engineer, and well suited for that position, being an MIT graduate aeronautical engineer. He seems to be a shy man, but you don't gain a lifetime of test and research flying, then follow that with a prestigious position with Lockheed-Georgia by being shy. A longtime Herk tester, Carl can count among his accom-

plishments at Lockheed the first human pickup by an HC-130H when on May 3, 1966, he made the live Fulton snatch of Capt. Gerald Lyvere, USAF; he then repeated it with a ''doubleheader'' by simultaneously retrieving Col. Allison C. Brooks, at that time the commander of the USAF Aerospace Rescue and Recovery Service (now, that's leadership!), and pararescue jumper A3c. Ronald Doll. Carl was also at the controls of the record-lifting DC-130H that carried four RPVs into the air in July 1976 — 44,510 pounds of external stores!

Carl loosens up, his ear-to-ear grin revealing his glee as he relates taking Leo Sullivan for the latter's first flight in the C-5. As the chief project pilot, Carl was quite proud of his giant charge. Everything had gone well — until the landing. The touchdown was routine, Leo placing the twenty-four-wheel main gear onto the Marietta runway as smoothly as you and I take the off ramp of the interstate at two in the morning. But when the nose gear settled, Katie, bar the door! A critical pivot pin was missing, either having dropped out or never having been installed prior to the flight, and the nose gear began a rapid series of ever-increasing shimmies, culminating in several complete 360-degree revolutions. Now, friends, when the nose gear on a

---

Lean and looking mean, Lockheed's shiny black HTTB (high technology test bed) is actually a research vehicle, currently testing STOL capabilities and fly-by-wire control systems.

Hercules' big brothers, the sleek C-141 Starlifter and the massive C-5 Galaxy, reflect the obviously beneficial design characteristics of the runt of the litter.

C-5 shimmies, that's industrial strength shimmy! The great airframe shook and tried to twist away from the grasp of Leo's big hands as it hurled down the runway, dipping and yawing and twisting.

Across the table from Carl, Leo joins in the laughter as Carl relates how he asked Sullivan what he was trying to do to "his" airplane. *Gee, let a guy fly it one time and he tries to break it!*

Carl, the veteran Hercules-Galaxy test and research pilot, has a new purpose in life now. The friendly, quiet, lifetime aviator will be a leading part of the team that will configure and test the HTTB — Lockheed-Georgia's high technology test bed, an extensively modified L-100-20 airframe. He obviously is quite proud of his role as he leads us through the lab where the new fly-by-wire mockup is being assembled and made ready for ground tests. He talks of how the system will undergo testing in the HTTB, when the team of young technicians will oversee the development of the system through a series of orderly, progressive tests, finally substituting the fly-by-wire technology for the more conventional hydraulically boosted systems of the C-130. Over his engineer's confidence, Carl betrays his pilot's instincts when he good-humoredly says, "They can have my rudder, and they can have my ailerons, but I keep my damn elevator!" *I'm with you, Carl!*

Carl leads me to Lockheed's simulator area, and we enter the darkened flight deck of a six-axis machine that can duplicate practically any of the forces and responses of a real aircraft. The instrument panel and control systems are of a generic four-engined airlifter. One of the project programmers slips in and takes the pilot's seat and turns on the heads-up display (HUD) for IFR navigation, approaches and landing. The system under development involves a projection of multicolored lines, circles, and triangles. Keep the proper shapes lined up and the simulator (read aircraft) will take you exactly where you have it programmed to take you. Want to touch down during zero-zero conditions precisely 636 feet beyond the numbers? Just fly the small triangles and you *will* touch down 636 feet beyond the numbers. We take a short flight and the reality is such that I find myself looking around for other aircraft and subconsciously brace myself as we flare for touchdown.

From the simulator area, we proceed over to the HTTB hangar, where the glossy black aircraft is undergoing some final work before the sched-

Three a month—forever? It seems that way as the demand continues for an airplane that has been in continuous production since 1954, the mighty Hercules.

uled roll-out the next day. Its innards are exposed where a number of inspection panels are off. The inside of the cargo compartment is a maze of wiring and technicians. The huge modified flaps are still in their jigs on the hangar floor. Work stands surround the Herk like an exterior skeleton.

"And you plan to roll this out tomorrow?" I ask.

Carl's grin spreads again. "Oh, it'll roll out on time. All we have to do is install some controls and button it up, really. No problem."

The twinkle in his eyes tells me more than his words. Next day, on schedule, the HTTB leaves the hangar.

Lockheed has a very simple philosophy: When you have something good, go with it. Nowhere has that philosophy been more apparent and successful than with their C-130 concept. The C-141 Starlifter and C-5 Galaxy are certainly much, much more than scaled-up Hercules, but the heritage is evident. That solid, hard-to-improve-upon basic design that caused all those eyebrows to raise when the prototype YC-130 was rolled from the hangar at Burbank is evident throughout the airlifter world — cavernous, straight-through cargo compartment; high wing; four engines; exterior-housed main gear; rear loading ramp.

To verify that, all you have to do is look not only at the C-141 and C-5 but at the world airlifter community as well. Douglas came out with the giant C-133 Cargomaster, first flown in 1956; then the YC-15 in 1975. Boeing, meanwhile, made an attempt to enter the assault airlift market with its YC-14, maiden flight August 9, 1976. While both the YC-14 and YC-15 were of a slightly different concept, STOL, they followed the Hercules basic design. This is not to say they were copies — far from it. Their overall design just reinforced the wisdom of the Lockheed engineers. Other countries also recognized the superb design that had spawned the C-130: Aeritalia came out with their twin-engined G222 Herk clone; the Soviet designs Anatov An-8, An-10, An-12, and An-22 all followed the C-130 concept. The An-72 did also, but it was more nearly a clone of the YC-14. The Spanish CASA Aviocar and Airtech Cn-235 use the same basic concept. De Havilland of Canada produced the smaller DHC-4 Caribou and the DNC-5 Buffalo, although De Havilland housed its retracted landing gear within the fuselage. Of course, the Fairchild 123 was a parallel development with the C-130 and may be thought of in some sense as a smaller two-engined Herk. The Soviet Ilyushin Il-76 is another example, closely resembling Lockheed's Starlifter. The Short Skyvan 3M can be thought of as a lightweight Hercules design, with twin engines and fixed gear. The Transall C-160 also recognizes the time-proven concept. And finally there is the massive Anatov An-124, the world's largest aircraft. It would

appear that any future heavy-lift cargo aircraft will be able to trace its ancestry back to the Hercules.

In the immediate future is the McDonnell-Douglas C-17. Designed to give a single capability to replace the two-step intertheater and then intratheater delivery of troops and cargo, the C-17 is an impressive design, a wide-bodied heavy lifter with external dimensions similar to the C-141 but with a bulk and weight capacity more near that of the C-5. Intended for small, austere airfield operation, the C-17 boasts an ability to turn around on a ninety-foot-wide runway and has a back-down capability for close-quarters ground maneuverability. Design and engineering projections indicate that it can carry a 168,000-pound payload into any strip that can take a Hercules with a 38,000-pound payload. Using propulsive lift capability developed during the YC-15 test program, the C-17 can approach the forward area landing zone at a steep angle, and its slow approach speed gives it an impressive short-field performance. Touted as the next generation airlifter, the C-17 prototye is now under construction and will, indeed, give an added dimension to our airlift forces.

The C-17, however, is more of a follow-on to the C-141 Starlifter than it is a Hercules replacement. While introduction of the C-17 into the airlift forces will enable many of the older C-130s to be retired, the Hercules fleet will remain a vital component in our overall airlift forces for years to come. The C-17 is not envisioned as a cost-efficient gunship; it will be too large and expensive a platform for such specialized tasks as Aerospace Rescue and Recovery, weather reconnaissance, Special Operations, and widespread use in polar research or USCG patrols. Even if it were made available for foreign procurement, its cost and size would not make it a suitable replacement for the versatile and economical Hercules.

For all of its confidence and faith in the Hercules and its continued growth, the Lockheed organization looks forward to the inevitable advances in airlifter development and procurement. In that future, there is always the possibility that marketing factors; cost of design, engineering, and production; and the realities of foreign competition will involve a multinational airlifter product. The European Airbus is an example of such a joint project in the passenger transportation field. It is highly successful and has made significant inroads into what has been an almost exclusively American market.

A consortium to design a multinational airlifter has already been formed, and Lockheed is a partner — along with Aerospatiale, British Aerospace, and Messerschmitt-Boelkow-Blohm — in the Future International Military/Civil Airlifter (FIMA) organization, which is looking ahead to the 1990s and early 2000s. While their conception of a twenty-first century airlifter is still in the speculative stage, the high-wing, four-engine, T-tail design prevalent in their current thinking also bears a striking resemblance to a "big-Herk," even to the use of propellers — counter-rotating swept props mated with advanced turbo-prop engines. Only slightly longer than the present L-100-30 Hercules, the FIMA aircraft has a significantly larger payload capacity and floor space.

John W. Sibley, Lockheed's FIMA program director, is an ex-USAF Herk jock who talks enthusiastically about Lockheed's participation in FIMA. A major voice, by virtue of experience and professional standing within the world aircraft production community, Lockheed intends to be in the fore in any multinational effort involving FIMA. Sibley is a big, ruggedly handsome, aggressive PR type with a practical background in airlifters. He is a confident salesman when he speaks of the applicability of the HTTB programs with respect to Lockheed's FIMA role. Like so many thousands of others, he is a dedicated Herculean.

And speaking of Herculeans . . .

We have met a number of enthusiastic Hercules aficionados in the foregoing pages: Leo Sullivan and Carl Hughes, two veterans of the entire Hercules development; Sam McGowan, the C-130 bombardier; Comdr. Jack Rector and his two VXE-6 new-generation C-130 crew members, Lieutenants Griffiths-Rossi and Erickson; S. Sgt. Ronald Martin of the AFRES, along with Major Buckhout and Lieutenant Redmond; Maj. Hernan Daguerre, the Argentine Herk driver; and M. Sgt. Robert E. Lee and the members of the weather crew out of Keesler Air Force Base. The list goes on and on to include all of the people who are a part of the C-130 community. But there are two more who deserve individual recognition.

The first is Lars Olausson, a Swedish Herculean who publishes a small booklet that lists every single Hercules ever made by serial number, purchaser, date of delivery, and history. His motivation is not profit; his booklet is modestly priced and is not a wide seller. But it is the result of an intense admiration of the Hercules and a sincere desire to follow the worldwide exploits of the namesake of the son of Zeus! When you

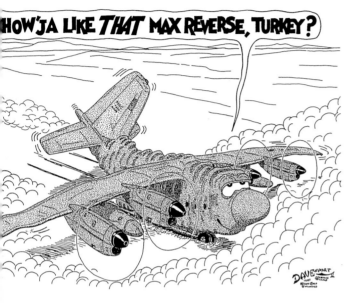

HOW'JA LIKE *THAT* MAX REVERSE, TURKEY?

toons annually graces a perfectly conceived calendar, and his drawings add humor to all sorts of other products such as T-shirts and ball caps.

But his real talent is his intimate and detailed knowledge of the development and history of the C-130. Bring up any Hercules story — *any* — and Dave Davenport will smile with recognition and more times than not add a new dimension or input to the tale. In the court of world opinion concerning the Lockheed C-130 Hercules, Dave Davenport must be considered an expert witness.

Such devotion to an inanimate object is shared by all of us, who in lesser or greater degrees take considerable pride in our role as Herculeans. There are those insensitive persons who maintain that one cannot love an inanimate object. They have obviously never watched an infant press a tattered blanket remnant to its face as it sleeps, nor have they really seen the flag of our country even though they may have glanced at it countless times. But if admiration, respect, and loyalty are part of that complex emotion we call love, then it is no trick to love Hercules.

And to airmen all over the world there is a special thrill in the sight of an ungainly looking C-130 breaking away from earth and pointing its overgrown proboscis toward the heavens. It is the same thrill that comes over us when we watch an ancient Ford Trimotor making a clattering pass in front of the Fourth of July air show crowd, or an overage DC-3 touching down on its tall, H-strutted landing gear, or a pair of restored P-51s swooshing by, their passage just a moment or two ahead of the smooth roar of their Rolls Royce Merlin engines.

It's a thrill one just can't put into words. Suffice it to say: We love ya, Herk.

realize that Olausson's very complete publication depends largely upon the input of fellow Herculeans all over the world, you can understand how devoted and widespread the C-130 fan club really is.

And finally, mention must be made of Dave Davenport, perhaps the number one fan of Hercules. Sitting in his small office on Pope Air Force Base, Dave, a retired USAF staff sergeant and former C-130 flight engineer, spends almost all of his nonwork time advocating the cause of Hercules. A base illustrator, he is an accomplished cartoonist and is known worldwide within the Hercules community for his ability to capture the personality and achievements of Hercules as well as its foibles. His Herky Bird series of car-

Appendix: C-130 Major Derivatives

C-130A

		Primary user
AC-130A	Gunship	USAF
C-130D	Ski-equipped transport	USAF
RC-130A	Photomapper	USAF
JC-130A	General test bed/missile tracking	USAF
GC-130A	Grounded DC-130A — test aircraft	USAF
DC-130A	Drone launcher and director	USAF/USN

C-130B

RC-130B	Elint (electronic intelligence)	USAF
LC-130F	Ski-equipped	USN
KC-130F	In-flight refueler	USMC
HC-130B	Search and rescue	USCG
JC-130B	Missile tracker/test bed	USAF
NC-130B	Boundary layer control research	USAF[1]
WC-130B	Weather observation	USAF

C-130E

MC-130E	Special Operations forces	USAF
AC-130E	Gunship	USAF
DC-130E	Drone launcher/director	USAF
HC-130E	Combat rescue/Fulton recovery	USAF[2]
EC-130E	Airborne battlefield command post	USAF[3]
EC-130G	Communications platform	USN
EC-130Q	Communications platform	USN
WC-130E	Special Operations forces	USAF

C-130H

AC-130H	Gunship	USAF
KC-130R	In-flight refueler	USMC
WC-130H	Weather reconnaissance	USAF
LC-130R	Ski-equipped	NSF[4]
JC-130H	Test bed	USAF
C-130K	Military airlifter	UK-RAF
HC-130H	Search and rescue	USAF/USCG
HC-130N	Helicopter tanker	USAF
HC-130P	Tanker/search and rescue variant	USAF
MC-130H	Special Operations	USAF
C-130H-30	Fuselage stretched 180 inches	USAF[5]

[1] Later assigned to NASA for earth resource task.
[2] Fulton removed. Designated MC-130E Combat Talon.
[3] Later reengined and designated EC-130H.
[4] Owned by National Science Foundation. Maintained and flown by U.S. Navy in antarctic operations.
[5] The RAF also flies the equivalent of the HC-130H-30, having designated their aircraft C.MK3s.

L-100	Civilian cargo carrier
L-100-20	Civilian cargo carrier (100-inch fuselage stretch)
L-100-30	Civilian cargo carrier (180-inch fuselage stretch)

There have been a number of one-of-a-kind or special use modifications such as the C-130H-MP maritime patrol aircraft used by Indonesia and the Saudi Arabian C-130HP automobile transport and C-130HS flying hospital, but these are not considered to be major derivatives.

About the Author

M. E. Morris served as a naval aviator for thirty years, retiring with the rank of captain. Currently a consultant on naval affairs and a lecturer on experimental aviation and on Antarctica, he has built and flies his own acrobatic aircraft. Morris is author of two novels, ALPHA BUG and THE ICEMEN. He lives in Colorado Springs.

1374 6192